Market Entropy

Market Entropy

How to Manage Chaos and Uncertainty for Improving Organizational Performance

Rajagopal

BEP BUSINESS EXPERT PRESS

Market Entropy: How to Manage Chaos and Uncertainty for Improved Organizational Performance

Copyright © Business Expert Press, LLC, 2020.

Cover image licensed by Ingram Image, StockPhotoSecrets.com

Cover and interior design by Exeter Premedia Services Private Ltd., Chennai, India

First published in 2020 by
Business Expert Press, LLC
222 East 46th Street, New York, NY 10017
www.businessexpertpress.com

ISBN-13: 978-1-95152-788-4 (paperback)
ISBN-13: 978-1-95152-789-1 (e-book)

Business Expert Press Marketing Collection

Collection ISSN: 2169-3978 (print)
Collection ISSN: 2169-3986 (electronic)

First edition: 2020

10 9 8 7 6 5 4 3 2 1

Printed in the United States of America.

With love to Arati

Abstract

Market entropy in not an unusual phenomenon in rapidly changing market ecosystem. Consumer preferences, market demand, and business models change with the advancement of innovation, technology, and social clause and lifestyle. Consequently, large markets that attracted huge demand for products and services eventually fragment and narrow down to minimum viable segments (niche market). The longitudinal and latitudinal factors affect market entropy. Today is caused due to chaos in entry and exit of firms, partial laissez-faire conditions in transitional destinations, and rapid growth in innovation and technology affecting consumer behavior. Chaos theory highlights nonlinear behavior and temporal dynamics in the process of replacing old and established technologies with the newly created ones and drives market competition. This book discusses competitive market dynamics that explain contextual market entropy caused because of swift changes in the innovation and technology scenarios. This book delineates the attributes of cognitive ergonomics of consumers responding to the market dynamics and discusses how consumers make behavioral adjustments under the shrinking scenarios of large markets. Finally, discussions in the book address preemptive strategies to manage chaos in markets. Multiplicity of marketing functions like manufacturing and distribution significantly has contributed to the chaos in the market. Increase in the market competition commonly induces fragmentation of demand and chaos among consumers, and drives companies to take tactical actions than simply following strategic approaches to control the market dynamics.

Keywords

entropy; market competition; chaos; consumer behavior; innovation; technology; market dynamics; cognitive ergonomics; business modeling

Contents

Preface

The most challenging task in managing a business is setting an order of functions among the various role players to gain strategic and tactical advantage in the competitive marketplace. The order of functions in the business process encompasses management of sustained consumer preferences, terms of references of suppliers, manufacturing deals, and retailer perspectives. In addition, many non-controllable elements, including politico-business implications, economic policies, societal values, technological growth, and legal directives, that affect business operations create disruptions in business. Thus, in a marketplace, entropy controls functional dynamics and often turns business operations complex. Entropy in market takes place due to lack of order or predictability, which leads to gradual decline into disorder. Such market condition affects attributes of competition, managerial decision-making process, organizational performance, and construing behavioral perspectives of consumers.

Market trends and consumer behavior are continuously changing, and social media are playing a critical role in determining marketing decisions. However, when uncertainty caused by entropy dominates, understanding the market volatility is vital. Volatility of consumer markets can have significant negative effects on risk-averse market share, profitability, and brand equity of companies. However, volatility is one of the most important concepts in the competitive growth theory. The central argument to this theory is that the companies operating in a competitive business environment consider consumer preferences, innovation, technology, and growth-related investments. The analysis of entropy in consumer markets can be regarded as the extension of both the information and probability theory. For the last two decades, it has become a very important measure for designing market and product portfolio and pricing techniques. A market appears to be a significant platform to visualize entropy and evaluate the performance of elements of marketing-mix and consumer behavior. The relationship between value and price influence the market. However, markets remain far from equilibrium, as consumer behavior stays unpredictable, causing entropy in the marketplace.

Entropy in markets today is commonly caused due to chaos in the entry and exit of firms, partial *laissez faire* conditions in transitional destinations, and rapid growth in innovation and technology, affecting consumer behavior. The chaos theory highlights nonlinear behavior and temporal dynamics in the process of replacing old and established technologies with the newly created ones and drive market competition. Abrupt launch of new products and withdrawal of existing products in view of innovation and technology boom triggers market entropy and chaos in consumer cognition. Looking beyond innovation and technology, shifts from the single-retailer model to a multi-retailer model has boosted market competition, which has affected market stability. Multiplicity of marketing functions like manufacturing and distribution significantly has contributed to the chaos in the market. Chaos and market entropy can be visualized in the mobile phone industry of China, which focuses on one supplier and one bounded retailer rationale. Accordingly, the single-retailer model is extended to a multi-retailer approach, which has augmented the market competition manifold. The consequence of such strategy has prompted chaos and competition among retailers, which has increased the possibility of intra-company brand cannibalization within the market. Increase in the market competition commonly induces fragmentation of demand and chaos among consumers and drives companies to take tactical actions than simply following strategic approaches to control the market dynamics. Consumers exhibit forward-looking behavior for demand-based pricing under the influence of social interactions, which often create chaotic perception among consumers and make it difficult for the managers to develop right strategies. In fact, the interplay of consumers within the digital platforms today also contributes to chaotic demand dynamics.

In the growing market chaos in the business-to-consumer and business-to-business market segments, managerial decisions against market uncertainties are becoming prominent in the global and local marketplaces. Managers' behavior under uncertainty contains disruptive elements such as adjusting or fragmenting the decision process into small steps, reducing uncertainty through learning market competition, building relationships with key players in the marketplace to avoid unforeseen changes, and taking ineffective decisions. Chaos in the market also induces uncertainty through negative communications on social media. Experience sharing by consumers about new brands on social media develops instable perceptions among consumers, which leads to brand uncertainty. Such cognitive disposition of consumers affects brand attitudes and preferences, and consequently affects brand performance. Therefore, market chaos demonstrates fragmented segments for brands to grow in niche. In competitive markets, where chaos prevails, managers are actively engaged in either preventing brand uncertainty or managing its post-effects on the consumer decision process. The discussion model of the book is exhibited in Figure P.1.

It is evident from the preceding attributes of market chaos why managers should understand the phenomenon of market entropy and learn strategic management methods to address the fundamental issues related to market disorders (entropy). In order to address the phenomenon of market entropy and the associated causes and effects, this book discusses decision modeling, new approaches of managing visual and hidden market fragmentations, interpreting market competition and consumer perspectives, and deriving right managerial touchpoints. Accordingly, this book identifies the strengths and weaknesses of the managerial decision-making process under the conditions of entropy and suggests developing innovative business models with an alternative thinking to sustain in chaotic markets.

This book discusses the causes and effects of market chaos, from statistical taxonomy of research studies to cognitive mapping of consumers over time in the global marketplace across consumer products industries. The book analyzes the emerging theory of *chaos*, fragmentation of markets, and developing agile business models to gain leverage in the competitive marketplace. The concepts and models developed in the book are central to market entropy, which are interpreted in terms of current consumer marketing and multi-brand management issues of companies across market destinations. The focus is on penetration of innovation through social networks as an autocatalytic process that generates multiple market niches. The book deliberates upon factors critical to the success of firms, which include diversity and cross-functionality, by reducing the impact of

Market competitiveness, business modeling, controlling entropy, minimum viable segments, rebuilding corporate, social and consumer values

Rules of engagement in marketing, combatting at grassroots, controlling value erosions, setting new market order, market consortium, consumer sovereignty

Current business ecosystem
- Shifting consumer preferences
- Increasing market competition
- Uncertainty in business performance
- Disruptive innovation
- Rapid growth in technology
- Influence of social media
- Consumer empowerment
- Loyalty dilemma

Managerial decision
- Consumer analytics
- Consumer centric business models
- Cocreation
- Decision uncertainties
- Strategies vs tactics
- Market leadership
- Securing market and controlling entropy

Conditions of market entropy
- Liberal entry and exit of firms
- Chaos in marketplace
- Market fragmentation
- Consumer dissonance
- Frequent mergers and acquisitions
- Closures or diversifications in business
- Agility in business vs corporate goals
- Vulnerability in market operations
- Business diplomacy and socio-political dynamics
- Shifts in industry attractiveness

Discussion platform, critical analysis and arguments
- Interpreting chaos theory in consumer markets
- Market transitions and geo-demographic fragmentation
- Decision process, loop, and disruptions
- Analyzing cognitive ergonomics,
- Strategy touchpoints in market operations
- Defensive marketing
- Market lifecycle

Discussions Paradigm

Analytical learning on market chaos, decision-making, and business agility

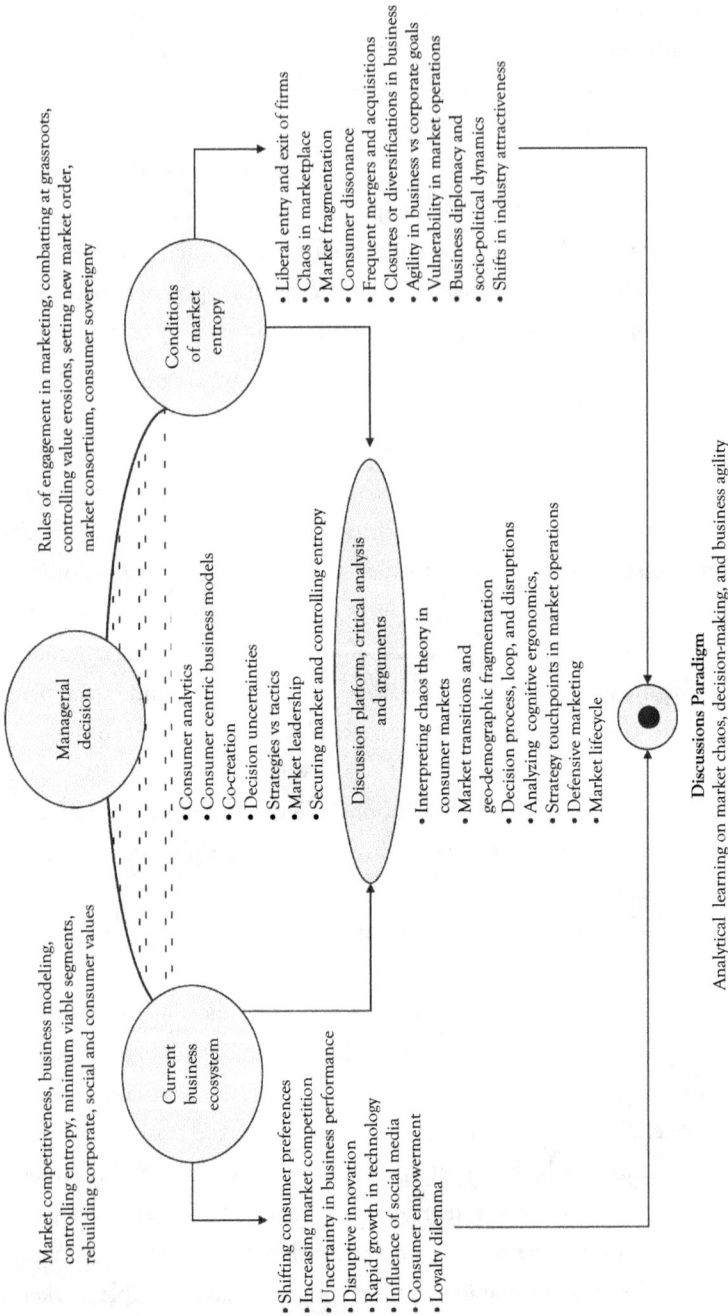

Figure P.1 Discussion paradigm of the book

Source: Author

market chaos. It is argued in the book that timely deployment of stream-lined marketing strategies in chaotic markets could reduce the effects of 3Ds comprising disruptive innovation, defection among consumers, and diminishing market share.

Major arguments in the book synthesize that chaos in communications technology causes chaos in consumer market. Such combination has trig-gered multiple brands within the company and attracting many players in the industry to operate on same time launching brands with marginal differ-entiation causing chaos. This situation has aggravated today, causing market entropy by fragmenting markets, wherein consumers exhibit high defection index across brands. Such market entropy has raised the question on creat-ing brand loyalty, as consumers strategically prefer no mobile phone brand. This book presents new insights on developing hybrid business models using both aggressive and defensive marketing strategies to manage chaotic flairs across products and services in the market and toward managing behavioral complexities of consumers. The book guides managers on both marketing tactics and strategies to manage time, territory, target, thrust (competitive), and tasks pivoting around consumers and market competitiveness.

In a simplistic view, entropy in market may take place when a new brand is pushed into an existing two-brand market. Therefore, a defensive market-ing structure needs to be enforced in the market by analyzing the causes and effects of entropy. Often, the product overlap strategy used by companies to enhance their product line to gain consumer confidence and probable com-petitive advantage is responsible for market entropy, leading to cannibaliza-tion within the product line. Entropy is very common in the fashion industry. Fashion accessories and core fashion products have short lifecycle and are often affected by the creative disruption and changing social values and life-style. Entropy, thus, indicates the incidences of uncertainty and chaos in the market. Using this highly developed and commendable area of science as context, one can see how consumer markets suffer from the chaotic mindset.

Entropy does not seriously affect the economy and markets of small companies operating in niche markets. However, companies with large-scale manufacturing and marketing systems and increasing requirements of high quality and performance suffer from the consequences of market entropy. It can be an indispensable situation at times with more com-plex multi-brands, markets, and embedded consumer values. This book blends the complexities of multi-brand and multi-market paradigms to converge with effective business performance to reduce chaotic effects, decision imperfections, and augment consumer values. The book argues that companies need to consider a broader perspective to protect market entropy within the market for their products and support marketing decisions derived by understanding the consumer behavior. This book bridges the design perspectives of chaotic markets with applied marketing decisions, putting the consumer first in the business management process.

Understanding the causes and effects of chaos in the markets, companies need to understand how to gain an inner analytic edge to defend entropy and recover the market share. In this process, applying knowledge derived from antecedents could improve the bottom-line decisions. Though companies draw some competition-based decisions through numerous charts, checklists, and examples, the book suggests logical framework analysis and consumer-centered strategies for making sustainable decisions against market chaos, uncertainties, and value deterioration. This book specifically discusses the following entropy-related perspectives in consumer markets:

- Regulating entries and exits and reducing whiplashes with the powerful demand-profit matrix
- Fitting business into consumer protected model to reduce the effects of market entropy
- The ways companies can stay as first movers and reap competitive advantage by bridging aggressive and defensive business strategies
- Understanding cognitive ergonomics of consumers to regulate their drifts across brands and streamline loyalty through the theory of optimal distinctiveness and value creation.

This simple but reliable mechanism of physical science has been ruling market performance since the dawn of economic activity, and it acts regardless of our will and ideological preferences. In such sense, this book establishes a theoretical foundation to develop future decision models based on logical framework, cognitive mapping of consumers, and learning from competitive distress. Converging the principles of market entropy, the real marketplace economy is the major challenge addressed in this book. Through multidisciplinary discussions, this book connects managers to dynamic markets and to behavioral domain of all entities playing role in the marketplace and offers a strategic direction in making marketing decisions.

This book is divided into five chapters. *Chapter 1* explains such bidirectional dynamics in business in the context of Darwinism in the context of growing chaotic behavior of markets and shifts in consumer decision-making abilities. Discussions on attributes of market competition and taxonomy of market across geo-demographic segments, threats of cannibalization and ways of competitor learning are central to this chapter. Principal attributes of conventional markets with focus on complexities of niche markets and changing retailing and shopping behavior of consumers are discussed in *Chapter 2*. Shifts in consumer behavior and consumption patterns in a niche to the large markets have been discussed as simulated chaos. This section in the chapter argues that shifts in the consumer behavior in niche markets drive rapid changes across the geo-demographic segments, which leads to the market fragmentation and market entropy over time. In addition, this chapter discusses causes and effects of demand fragmentation, consumer defection, and price entropy. *Chapter 3* discusses the causes of innovation boom in consumer-centric and industrial products and its effects on market entropy. The chapter also addresses the attributes of incremental innovation, reverse innovation, and their changing market potential. Discussions are also central to the breakthrough innovations in the context of their market potential and effects on large markets in this chapter. The lifecycle of innovation in the context of market chaos and demand fragmentation has been discussed in the chapter to explain the concept of market entropy. The compatibility between cognitive attributes and the cognitive architecture in the socio-economic behavioral processes is discussed in *Chapter 4*. The behavioral factors contributed by the intrinsic and extrinsic factors are discussed in this chapter in the context of developing cognitive ergonomics. Perceptual mapping, semantics, and role of perceived values of consumers are discussed comprehensively in the following text. In addition, this chapter also discusses the new concept on cognitive anarchy and its implications on consumer behavior. Finally, *Chapter 5* discusses strategies for managing market chaos in the context of strategic differentiation, planning-organizing-collaboration, and market integration.

This book connects students, researchers, and managers with behavioral domain consumers, realities of markets, and their strategic evolution in the contemporary scenario. It serves as a quick guide to understand why large markets are shrinking and reasons behind entrepreneurs choosing minimum viable segments to operate business. The broad foundation of this book is laid on the conceptual discussions on consumer and market behavior. The book carries applied arguments toward consumer perceptions, cognition, and decision making in the context of consumer-centric markets. This book categorically reviews theories, concepts, and previous researches and discusses the applied tools and techniques to understand consumer behavior and the decision-making process. This book significantly contributes to the existing literature and serves as a learning post and a think-tank for students, researchers, and business managers. The elements are arranged in a pyramidal model with four kinds of interlinked discussions that include *behavioral developments* of consumers at the top followed by *competitive push* needed in marketing decisions, *functional performance* of the marketing decisions at the middle, and then *market entropy* at the bottom of the pyramid.

I have been teaching consumer behavior, marketing strategy, and international business management courses in MBA programs for over a decade, during which my knowledge, insights, and critical thought process have periodically updated. I found that market entropy has not been talked in any of these courses, as no textbooks have identified it as a topic of interest. In reality, we all realize that large markets are shrinking to regional grounds and later to niche markets. I felt it necessary to share with students the applied concepts of market entropy and cognitive ergonomics of consumers that affect the decisions at both levels of consumers and companies. Therefore, this book is an outgrowth of the thought process from a classroom to a wider platform of audience. I have taught the mentioned courses from the perspectives of delivering contemporary practices in marketing management to students, putting them through various real-life business scenarios so that they can analyze the market complexities and gain confidence in choosing the right strategies to do business in the competitive marketplace. New markets are emerging, growing, and fragmenting over time. This book aims at exploring the causes and effects of Darwinian fitness in the global marketplace and carrying out in-depth discussions into the new generation management involving stakeholders in developing customer-centric business strategies and understanding the right consumer cognition. This book argues advanced marketing-mix and several consumer-centric strategies to associate consumers as associates to co-create new businesses in new markets. Initially, I worked out a teaching agenda on strategic marketing and business expansion models for global companies and discussed them in length in the classroom, encouraging timeless discussions on the subject that helped in developing new conceptual frameworks on the subject. Some of my research papers on business modeling and customer-centric marketing in the emerging markets have been published in the international refereed journals, which had driven new insights on the subject. Accordingly, filtered and refined concepts and management practices have been presented in the book that are endorsed with applied illustrations and updated review of literature on managing business in the overseas destinations.

This book is a good fit for managers to learn the intricacies of market entropy and consumer behavior. It is also a notable learning resource for researchers and students of marketing strategy, marketing research, business analytics, and courses in decision sciences. This book has been developed to serve as a managerial guide and think-tank for the graduate students engaged in studying courses on business strategy and marketing. Besides serving as a reference book to the students, this would also be an inspiring book for managers, market analysts, and business consultants engaged in the decision-making process for developing a marketing strategy. I hope this book will contribute to the existing literature and deliver new concepts to the students and researchers to pursue the subject further. By reading this book, working managers may also realize how to converge best practices with corporate strategies in managing business at the destination markets, while students would learn the new dimensions of marketing strategies.

Rajagopal
Mexico City
January 01, 2020

Acknowledgments

In completing this volume of the book, I have been benefitted by the discussions of my colleagues within and outside EGADE Business School. I am thankful to Dr. Ernesto Amoros, Professor and Associate National Director of Doctoral Program at EGADE Business School, Mexico, who has given me the opportunity to deliver courses on Qualitative Research in the doctoral program. I thank all my students of graduate and doctoral programs at EGADE Business School for sharing enriching ideas on the subject during the classroom discussions, which helped in building this book on the framework of innovative ideas. This book is an outgrowth of my teaching new concepts in qualitative research to doctoral research scholars and working managers in the MBA program.

I also acknowledge the outstanding support of Robin J. Zwettler, Executive Editor of Business Expert Press, who critically examined the proposal, guided the manuscript preparation, and took the publication process forward. My special thanks to Dr. Naresh Malhotra, Regents Professor Emeritus at Scheller College of Business, Georgia Tec University, and series editor on consumer behavior subject at Business Expert Press, for his guidance and encouragement in bringing out this volume. I am thankful to various anonymous referees of my previous research works on innovation and technology management who helped me in looking deeper into the conceptual gaps and improving the quality with their valuable comments.

Though it was a solo journey with this publication project from ideation to manuscript preparation, I must acknowledge the encouragement from senior academics to proceed ahead with the project. I express my deep gratitude to my wife Arati Rajagopal who always reminded me of this task over other deadlines in the agenda. She also deserves kudos for copy editing the manuscript rigorously before submitting it to the publisher.

CHAPTER 1

Competitive Market Dynamics

Overview

Markets have evolved over time with the increase in market competition, which has stimulated companies toward continuous refinement in strategies. There has been a bidirectional growth of business across companies and regions in the past few decades, encouraging multinational companies to expand their markets into the bottom-of-the-pyramid consumer segments. Simultaneously, local companies have shown vigor to grow global over the years. The chapter explains such bidirectional dynamics in business in the context of Darwinism. The growing chaotic behavior of markets and shifts in consumer decision-making are central to the discussion in this chapter. Attributes and taxonomy of market competition, threats of cannibalization, and ways of competitor learning also constitute the core discussion in this chapter.

The evolution of markets over the centuries has been a perennial phenomenon congruent with the shifts in social, economic, and technological knowledge in the society. The evolution of business and growth has promoted bidirectional economic behavior to explore the markets. Sociologically, the evolution of markets is based on the understanding that individuals are embedded in various cognitive structures involving the business activities. Shifts in the market processes have induced fundamental beliefs and shared assumptions like entrepreneurial alliances and sharing cultural and ethnic values with large companies. Such business evolution paradigms are resistant to minor discrepancies between their fundamental models and the contradicting (potentially empirical) evidence. Thus, discrepancies in market behavior are considered as socio-economic abnormalities, paradoxes, or puzzles in a given place and time (Hedaa and Ritter 2005).

Darwinian Fitness in Marketplace

Darwinism refers to the evolution of biological life, but it can be analogically fit to the growth of global–local business, as multinational companies are penetrating down to remote geo-demographic areas, while local companies are recovering their strength to move out of niche and grow global. These bidirectional shifts symbolize the Darwinian principles of survival of the fittest (multinational companies exploring remote geo-demographic markets) and struggle for existence (local companies aiming to grow national, regional, and global). Therefore, Darwinism is becoming obvious in global markets and contemporary industrial revolution (Rajagopal 2012).

The concept of Darwinian fitness explains capturing of evolutionary dynamics among companies from developed and developing markets. It justifies that businesses of all generations have the tendency to expand geographically and adapt to new environments to exist in the global business cycle. The entrepreneurial traits for adaptation to new business environment can be understood as the business fitness, and more precisely, as *inclusive fitness* (West and Gardner 2013). Darwinian fitness in business is integrated with growth and performance and serves as a *business continuum*. Teleological growth in the business continuum can be viewed in the ultimate goal of a company *toward expanding its business for maximizing profit*. This refers to natural selection of the stages of evolution and corresponds to the principle of biological teleology (Mossio et al. 2009; Shapiro 2011). The behavioral ecosystem of companies adapting to Darwinism in business is based on the idea that change underlies the efforts to optimize the geo-demographic business. Accordingly, successful companies develop adaptation to the local business ecosystems. The collaboration of multinational companies with local companies helps in developing new business traits and induces them to naturally adapt to the ethnic strategies. Such strategies of large companies lead to better contribution to local market needs and overall business fitness (*e.g.*, Huneman 2019).

Historical documentation reveals that market evolution is a long process that enables some causal attribution (Goldthorpe 2000). Historical analysis can sometimes enable identification of the reasons for important transitions by highlighting the key events that triggered change and their patterns. Marketing patterns in the society are commonly believed to have evolved through five distinct phases of growth for ages. These phases can be categorized as the simple trade era, the production era, the sales era, the marketing department era, and the marketing company era (Rajagopal 2012). Continuous innovation and technology in the consumer products companies have set new trends in the market and created dynamic value perceptions among consumers, which has raised their preferences and expectations.

Digital marketing has opened massive opportunities to deliver new consumer experiences and strengthened the relationships with consumers across destinations in the global marketplace. Digital disruption has created new dimensions in consumer marketing to drive compulsive buying behavior through the benefits of large-scale promotions and convenience. Platform economy has shown a huge shift in creation of consumer value. The platform economy distinctly comprises a new set of business and economic relations that depend on the Internet, computation, and data. Consequently, the industrial revolution adapted to the technological progress and began to keep pace with the population. Such growth in the industrial products and services for consumption and business needs created new markets, and by the middle of the 19th century, the global transformation in product and financial markets were observed. The customer-centric marketing approaches gave an easy access to the multinational companies to develop latitudinal expansion of their business and penetrate the local markets. Accordingly, relationships with customers and global–local alliances have grown as critical success factors for multinational companies engaged in marketing. The increased interest in these concepts has triggered a paradigm shift from mass marketing toward relationship marketing. It has been observed by end of 20th century, and that only a relationship orientation secures firms' success (Hedaa and Titter 2005). The theories of social identity, persuasion, and multiculturalism have motivated global–local moves among the multinational companies to do business in the local geo-demographic market segments.

Ethnic marketing has the potential to reach the diverse consumer segments across regions and generational cohorts. Ethnicity attributes in marketing have driven the local enterprises to develop tie-up alliances with multinational firms. Ethnic marketing approaches develop a strong socio-cultural sensitivity that bridges the global–local differences in geo-demographic expansion of companies (Harrison et al. 2017; Licsandru and Cui 2019).

Business expansion has observed a phenomenal change in the global marketplace over the years, which resulted into the economic dynamism in both developed and developing economies of the countries across the continents. Accordingly, many countries jumped into the market fray and started to produce a larger variety of products, making them more substitutable, raising the price elasticity of demand, and strengthening competition. Such market development had driven higher competition to modern growth, and competitive firms aimed at larger territorial expansion at lower markups with prolonged break-even. As firms grow larger, they find it easier to cover the fixed cost on diffusion and adaptation of innovation and technology. As the size of the market is large with significant competitive driving force, the market innovation grows endogenously. This, in turn, pushes the market to grow exponentially, providing additional incentives to mount competition. The market economy, thus, moves in the global marketplace to the era of competition, which is consistent with the Darwinian theories of struggle for existence and survival of the fittest.

Darwinian fitness, in the context of business, can be explained as a continuous evolution of firms in vertical and horizontal dimensions. Vertical expansion of business firms occurs when they widen their product-mix across the product portfolios and increase the length of product-line within the portfolios. Firms expanding their business across the geo-demographic segments lead to horizontal expansion. Most multinational companies today are exploring the bottom-of-the-pyramid markets for establishing production and business operations to gain competitive benefits. To ensure fitness in the changing competitive market scenarios, firms regularly make decisions about expanding their businesses by exploring destinations, acquiring new technologies, enlarging their plants, and increasing the size of the human resources. Such business expansion has a direct effect on the firms' profits through reduction in the costs or by serving a larger group of customers. However, it may also have an indirect effect in signaling market conditions with potential competitors, and it helps in building customer loyalty and satisfaction in the chaotic market-place (Espínola-Arredondo et al. 2011). The various aspects of Darwinian fitness in the marketplace are illustrated in Figure 1.1.

Darwinian fitness in marketplace is contextual to the market ecosystem, corporate socialization to create societal and consumer value, and cognitive ergonomics among the consumers and market players, as illustrated in Figure 1.1. The market competition is inextricably linked to the consumer (human factors) ergonomics, perceived values, and user-centered consumption design. The cognitive ergonomics reflects the physical, cognitive and social needs, desire, satisfaction and values, quality of life perceptions, and goals of a person or team in the context of technology, environment, and culture, which enable consumers to associate with brands and companies in the marketplace (Lawler et al. 2011). Cognitive ergonomics focuses on the relationship of products and services with the cognitive capabilities of users. It draws on the knowledge of human perception, mental processing, and memory. Chaos among consumers causes unregulated flow of products carrying innovations with a disruptive edge. Such operational environment damages cognitive ergonomics of the consumers. Multinational companies are exploring consumer markets at the bottom-of-the-pyramid with a view to expand their businesses and explore new consumer experiences by widening mass-market operations in the low-end segments. These companies tend to achieve these goals through mergers and acquisitions of local companies, manufacturing using intermediate technology, and low-cost innovation. Most customer-centric multinational companies like IKEA follow co-designing strategies for products to create customer value. Such corporate behavior at the low-end market segments is built around social and ethnic values that help companies inculcate brand emotions and consumer surplus over brands of the competing firms. By the mid-1990s, most multinational companies manufacturing consumer products have penetrated the remote markets of developing countries, and many have suffered from the low-end market syndrome causing high sales and low profit due to low-pricing strategy. Therefore, these companies suffer from one of the Darwinian doctrines of *survival of the fittest*, as exhibited in Figure 1.1.

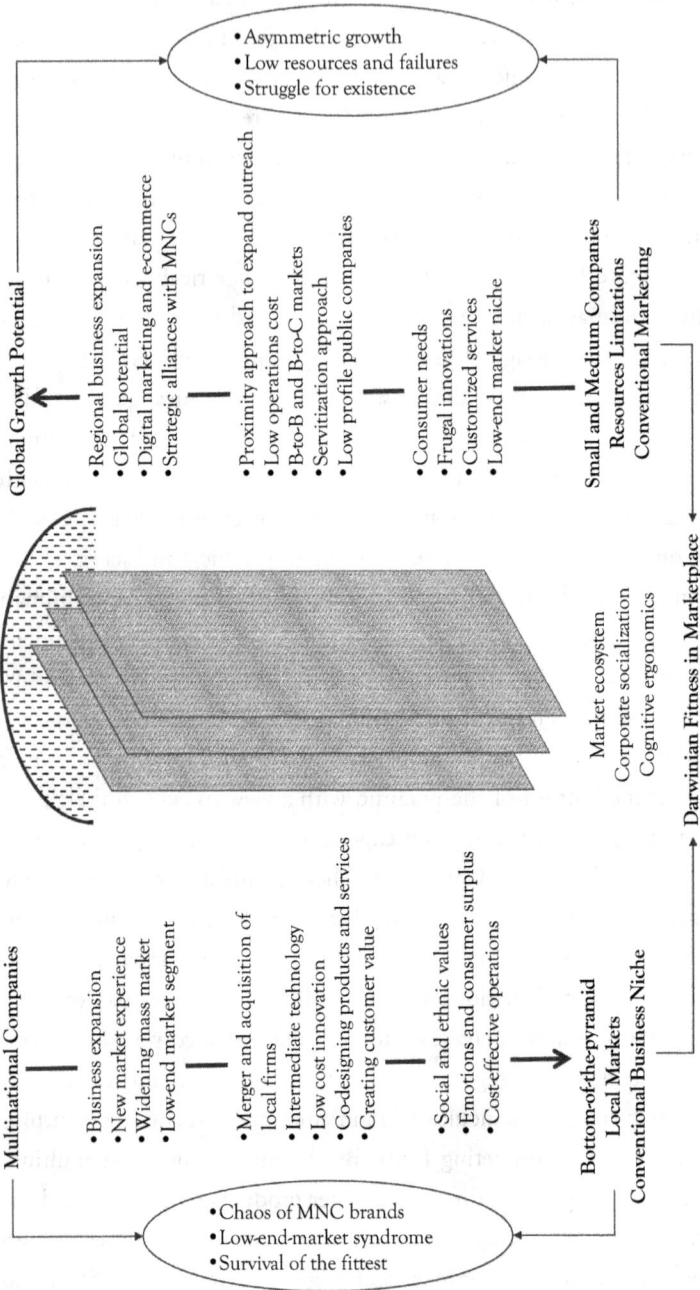

Figure 1.1 Bidirectional perspectives of Darwinian fitness in marketplace

Source: Author

In another scenario, the small and medium enterprises growing in local market, which have low resources and follow conventional marketing practices, are aiming to break their niche and expand their business operations, as shown in Figure 1.1. The local companies adapt to frugal innovation based on the consumer needs and prefer to operate within niche. These companies follow proximity approach (assessing demand in neighboring markets) to move out of niche. Local firms stay popular among the customers as they follow the servitization approach at low operations costs. Most local firms also serve large industries as suppliers or feeder firms within the geographic limits. Often, such business relationship of local firms with large companies gives them an opportunity to grow regional and develop strategic alliances with the multinational companies. However, these firms observe asymmetric growth due to streamlined business planning and low resources and often face failure (sometimes, irrecoverable losses). Therefore, despite various financial and organizational limitations, the local firms aim to grow global and face many turnarounds in their journey, which conforms to another Darwinian dictum of *struggle for existence*. In this way, the business today has bidirectional dynamics in business growth that explains Darwinism in the business.

In the growing market competition, small firms always face major threat from large firms, as the latter possess more resources such as physical infrastructure, finance, human resources, and technology. Most of the smaller firms, unable to continue their struggle for existence in the marketplace, develop cocooning attitude and confine to a niche. Often, large firms enter new market niches created by small firms through technological innovation and ingest the market share of small firms. In view of the Darwinian theory, market conditions and company-specific characteristics explain entry timing and the underlying goals of the large firms, and such entry might be a continuous process for large firms in different marketplaces. The dominating behavior of large firms is more likely to be backed by the incremental and reverse innovations. Small firms are affected by entry of the firms that are similar in size and resources. When a company enters the new market, it raises the probability of surviving solely on its market attractiveness (Debruyne and Reibstein 2005). Therefore, small firms play aggressive and defensive strategies to stay in the marketplace, despite the competitive attacks by new entrants. However, consortium of small firms manufacturing identical products also poses a major threat to large firm in sustaining the competitive marketplace.

The top-down (global to local) and bottom-up (local to global) market competitions among firms induce chaotic behavior among firms, stakeholders, and consumers. The higher concentration of large firms in the local markets overrides the natural market competition at the bottom of the pyramid and worsens the outcomes such as higher prices and increase in credit transactions and cost of workforce for market participants. Therefore, the organizational triad of *structure–conduct–performance* of small firms is adversely affected (Scott and Dunkelberg 2010). Small firms operating in the regional niche markets are successfully transforming their businesses to adapt to the fast-changing competitive landscape using contemporary technologies and customer-centric marketing strategies. However, the pace of their transformation to compete with the large incumbents is slow, which appears to be one of the major causes for their struggle to survive (Turner and Endres 2017). Such situation is contextual to one of the Darwinian maxims that explains the *struggle for existence* phenomenon.

The rapid growth in trade and economy across the global marketplace has stimulated the manufacturing and services industries and triggered a chaotic market competition among large companies. Market competition turned hybrid from 1980s onward, as both e-commerce and brick-and-mortar stores co-existed in the marketplace. The growth in technology used by the large companies augmented consumers' interest over online purchases, which contributed to the increased business stress and competition in local markets, affecting small businesses within and outside their community (Giaglis and Fouskas 2011). In a non-theoretical scenario, large companies tend to override small businesses in the local markets and tend to either eliminate them or offer the proposals of mergers or acquisitions. Such behavior of firms does not advocate a healthy market competition; it rather exhibits the attributes of business power and cannibalization. This phenomenon conforms to the Darwinian principles of *struggle for existence* and *survival of the fittest*. Some small firms stand out in the crowd and compete with the international business corporations. Mirc Electronics, a medium-sized consumer electronics company in India, commenced its journey in 1981 against the Japanese and Korean consumer electronics companies. Starting with a goal of manufacturing televisions sets of Onida brand, it transformed into a complete consumer durable company, with a wide product portfolio, including flat panel TVs (LED LCD TVs), air conditioners, washing machines, microwave ovens, DVD home theater systems, mobile phones, projector systems, and LED lights, over the years. This company exports these products to Middle Eastern and North African (MENA) market. This company stands as an example of Darwinian fitness in the global market.

Generally, small businesses with a smaller customer base and fewer resources acquire low market power. These companies stay vulnerable to external market changes (Cowling et al. 2015). Therefore, small businesses tend to cut down investments to avoid risks and view market competition unenthusiastically. These companies emerge as start-up enterprises in a niche and innovate or co-create products in association with stakeholders and consumers, but fail to commercialize them. Large companies with a commercialization plan specific to such innovations acquire innovations or the company and develop global marketing strategies for these reverse innovations. Cost and marketability drive the strategy of reverse innovation. Large companies, thus, roll over to the local markets to identify the customer-centric innovations developed by the local enterprises and tend to evaluate the economics of their business projects. Commercializing reverse innovation is a disruptive leap to hit a product in the target market, and it demands to develop organizational insight into how a new product could drive an impact in an emerging market. GE Healthcare has demonstrated this idea with the customization of its low-cost ultrasound and electrocardiogram machines, which started as emerging market products and then evolved into valuable devices for North America and Europe (Rajagopal 2016).

Darwinian fitness in market evolution argues that when the consumers' choices increase, more varieties of products and services penetrate the market, driving more demand. Such market thrust in positioning products and services increases the price elasticity of demand. Some management studies exploit this feature and show in a one-period model how the higher elasticity of demand, due to a larger population or more liberalized trade, facilitates innovation (Desmet and Parente 2010). As the trade liberalization continued in the global marketplace, transforming the regional markets, the multidimensional growth appeared to be a strong catalytic thrust in the economy of developing countries. The multidimensional growth, in which a corporate firm manages relatively free-standing business units, was the most successful design of the marketing organizations of the 20th century. However, some firms have evolved organizational designs that signal a new way of resolving the market competition. These firms are organized around multiple dimensions, such as region, product, services, and account, that are able to hold different strategies accountable for performance on these dimensions. The multidimensional growth of marketing organization is best understood as the next step in the evolution from a resource-centric business model to a customer-centric knowledge-sharing model. It is a way of managing competitive markets that is particularly well adapted to stimulating the market leadership that is necessary to create economic value in complex markets (Strikwerda and Stoelhorst 2009).

Market Chaos

Continuous innovation and technological development are the main sources of core competitiveness in the marketplace. Frugal innovations at the low-end markets create chaos in a business, as consumers have several options to make buying decisions, while most end up in the confusion or chaotic decisions. The technological content is an important factor of innovative products, which might provide clarity of information among consumers and help in making the right decision. Frugal innovations offer low-cost benefits, but cause unpredictable consumer defections. Firms that have the optimal technological contents might draw profits and overcome chaotic market effects (Li and Wang 2019). The chaotic market behavior emerges from unorganized market competition, liberal entries of firms in the marketplace, lack of organizational control, and business governance. Market chaos is often described as unpredictable and random when observed over the long term. Chaotic behavior of firms in the market is often caused by rolling out low-end products in the mass consumer segment and stimulating demand on low-price and high-promotion tactical grid. The chaotic business situations not only affect the market ecosystem, but also damage the organizational design of the companies (Houry 2012).

The theory of chaos has been the topic of interest in physical sciences, but it has also proved significant in financial and business management sciences in the context of growing competition today. The chaos theory has been explained in previous studies on financial theory and practice and management of competition in the marketplace. In the course of growing instability and increasing role of randomness in commodity and consumer markets, attention to this theory is growing in the area of streamlining the managerial decision-making. In this connection, it is important to determine the possibilities and limits of chaotic moves in the customer-centric and business-to-business markets across financial transactions and products and services marketing (Klioutchnikov et al. 2017).

Chaos is a natural phenomenon in any dynamic state of action, unless it is regulated or controlled through the set principles of action. The chaos theory has emerged as a field of study in mathematics, with applications in several disciplines, including meteorology, sociology, physics, engineering, economics, biology, and philosophy. Of late, this theory has also been interpreted meticulously in business, as it leads to various uncertainties in market competition. The chaos theory studies the behavior of dynamic systems that are highly sensitive to initial conditions, a paradigm popularly referred to as the butterfly effect. In reference to business, the butterfly effect drives through small changes in marketing-mix, corporate policies, organizational culture, and competitive strategies, which leads to larger effects in stimulating market share, business growth, and acquiring and retaining customers. Chaos in market is commonly caused due to congestion of competitors, frequent introduction and withdrawal of products and services, and extensive price promotions. Small differences yield widely diverging outcomes in dynamic market systems, often rendering long-term prediction, generally impossible in a market or a business. This happens even though the market systems that are deterministic, which means that their future behavior is fully determined overruling the uncertainties. In consumer markets, the chaos is frequent, and these markets are very susceptible to the butterfly effects. In consumer markets, the chaos and butterfly effects are very popular in fashion products and consumer electronics (Rajagopal 2015).

It has been observed that the spatial and temporal complexities in a market have emerged due to frugal innovations, geo-demographic expansion of mass-market, and increasing low-end market competition. This situation is aligned with Darwinian principles that suggest managing *the unexpected* (Weick and Sutcliffe 2001) and competing *on the edge of chaos* (Brown and Eisenhardt 1998). The chaos theory has, thus, entered the spotlight of organization and management studies in exploring chaos in consumer behavior, production and business operations, and managing primary market. Accordingly, the chaos theory explains unpredictable consequences, as cause is not linearly proportional to the eventual effect. Sometimes, a subtle error is dramatically amplified far from the market equilibrium, as the nonlinear dynamic system behaves across time. For example, in the mobile phone industry, the boom of android system mobile communication devices created an unpredictable chaos in both the industry and the market, while the products of Apple Inc. stayed out of the chaos being highly distinctive. In the recent development, launch of mobile phones by the Xiaomi Corporation (China) has made an unpredictable move in the low-end portfolio market with distinctive features. The success stories of Apple Inc. (high-end market) and Xiaomi (low-end market) explains the ways to differentiate products to stay unaffected by the market chaos. A business must deliver its promises and express genuine concern for its customers. Organizations must be designed to facilitate interaction with those who buy its products or services. All interactions from product design and sales transaction to post-sale activities, including delivery, installation, training, maintenance, warranty, and repurchase, need to be implemented with passion, respect, and trust (Shih et al. 2014). Such customer-centric behavior of companies helps them stay out of chaos and build *design-to-perform* paradigms.

The success of any innovation, which has been the target for the mass market, may trigger the market chaos, as fierce competition begins at the low-end markets. Such competition diverts consumers from the principal brands and helps the companies acquire consumers to low-price utilitarian or social status products. The growth of virtual channels would also drive the competition and chaos in the market. Market chaos at the low-end markets is generally prompted by the local companies, which gives way to international and virtual companies to push through the marketspace.

On the contrary, chaos in the high-end market occurs due to the rush of identical products by high-priced brand icons. Such competition at the high-end markets fragments the market share of the companies and drives most consumers to adapt to the fashion consumption behavior without developing loyalty for any brand. Many firms that enter with one-touch technology fall into the high-end market chaos (Rajagopal 2015).

Chaotic market behavior is predictable for a while and then becomes random, driving consumers in a dilemma to respond to the uncertain marketing strategies of the companies. The companies that would like to have a leapfrog experience in the competition by earning higher market share applying price-driven tactics often initiate chaos in the market. Under such market conditions, companies experience high uncertainties and are unable to develop strategic plans. Thus, embracing chaos seems the opposite of discipline and planning. However, uncertainty is embedded in negotiations, and the negotiators who ignore this fact and follow rigid strategies blind themselves to unexpected threats and slip potential opportunities (Wheeler 2004). Small companies pursue their technological goals at a local level over many years, staying cost-effective and combating with uncertainty and operations setbacks. Consequently, these companies tend to adapt their products quickly to meet the market needs. By contrast, many managers of large organizations emphasize on orderly and predictable operations in the context of strategic goals. Innovative large companies sometimes accept the market realities in developing innovative process and behave much like their smaller counterparts. Such moves also create chaos, but remain obscure (Quinn 1985). The ecosystem of market chaos is exhibited in Figure 1.2.

Chaos in the market is usually an unpredictable phenomenon. It occurs due to isolated and cross-effects of several short-term and strategic factors, as illustrated in Figure 1.2. The common marketing strategies of competing firms that cause chaos in the market include frugal innovations, price competition, liberal entry and exit of firms, multichannel marketing of identical and similar products, low-end substitution, and penetration of brands of multinational companies in local markets. These factors drive chaos among the market players, consumers, and stakeholders, as the market share is asymmetrically divided among competing companies. In addition, aggressive brand promotions, extensive franchising,

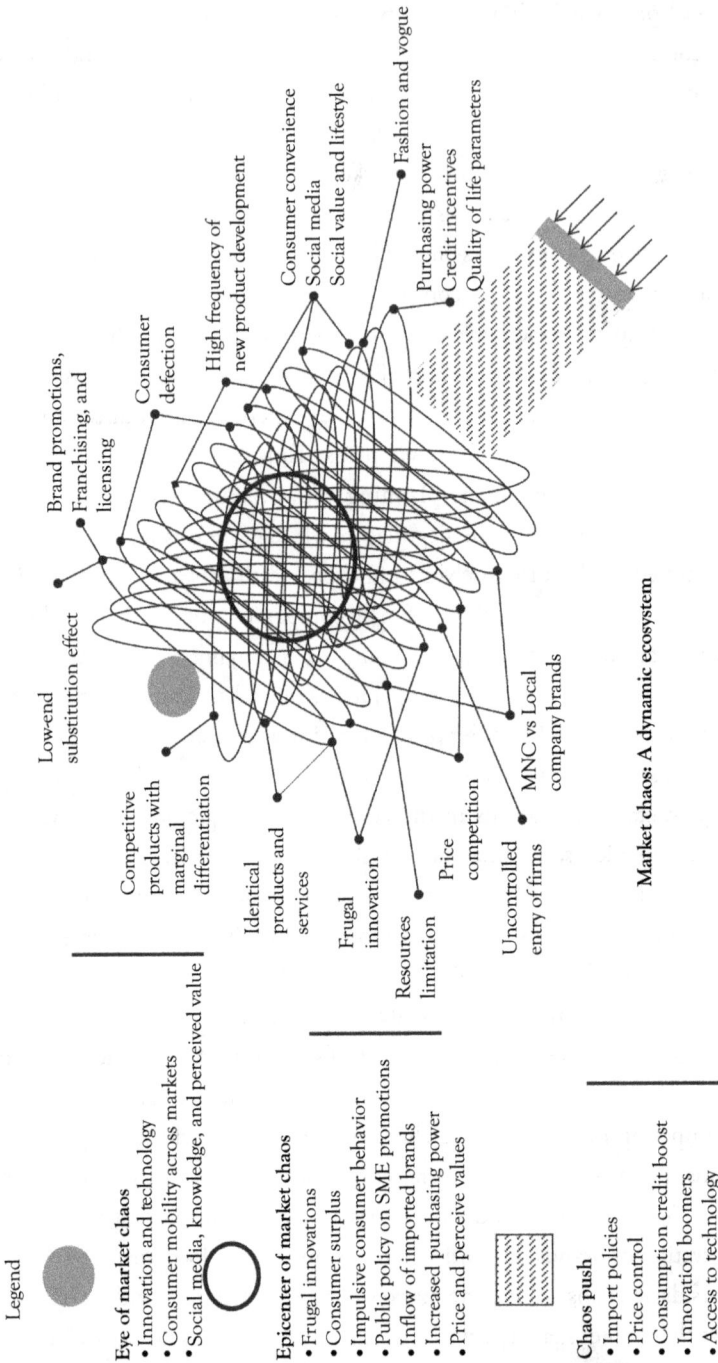

Figure 1.2 Dynamism of market chaos

Source: Author

Legend

Eye of market chaos
• Innovation and technology
• Consumer mobility across markets
• Social media, knowledge, and perceived value

Epicenter of market chaos
• Frugal innovations
• Consumer surplus
• Impulsive consumer behavior
• Public policy on SME promotions
• Inflow of imported brands
• Increased purchasing power
• Price and perceive values

Chaos push
• Import policies
• Price control
• Consumption credit boost
• Innovation boomers
• Access to technology

Brand promotions, Franchising, and licensing

Consumer defection

High frequency of new product development

Consumer convenience
Social media
Social value and lifestyle

Fashion and vogue

Purchasing power
Credit incentives
Quality of life parameters

Low-end substitution effect

Competitive products with marginal differentiation

Identical products and services

Frugal innovation

Resources limitation

Price competition

Uncontrolled entry of firms

MNC vs Local company brands

Market chaos: A dynamic ecosystem

and licensing of consumer brands (food, textile, electronics, and so on) and services cause chaos in the market not only due to excessive competition, but also due to the immense consumer defection. Consumer convenience and social media also contribute to the cognitive disruptions and instability in consumer decisions. The epicenter of market chaos is built by the excess inflow of frugal innovations, products with low-cost intermediate technology, and low-price products in the markets. Products and services provide concurrent value for money to consumers; they also generate significant demand in the low-end markets, resulting into impulsive consumer behavior. In addition, the public policies in the developing economies offer several financial incentives to the small and medium enterprises, which triggers market congestion of low-end products and services in the niche markets. Large companies exploring low-end segments further overcrowd the market with the products and services at competitive prices. In this way, the effects of public policy and intervention of large companies in the low-end market segments create the forced oligopolistic market situation.

Similarly, chaos in market also occurs in the high-end market, as many brands penetrate the premium consumer segment with high-technology and high-price products. Examples may be cited of hybrid automobiles, green and health conscious consumption products, apparel and fashion accessories, and perfumery products. The import policies that allow foreign brands to penetrate the market significantly push the chaotic market behavior. For instance, the Mexican market is open to the North American consumer companies, and Asian products from China, Thailand, and India enter the market through North American supply chain. Consumption credit boost is another major reason in building consumption chaos, as consumers gain manifold increase in their purchasing power because of the easy credit availability.

Chaos in the global as well as local markets has been caused since 1980 across the developing economies, due to introduction of new products as an outgrowth of continuous innovation and growth in technology, free entry and exit of firms, frequently changing consumer preferences, and high substitution effects that make the trust and loyalty of consumers fragile. Chaos in market prompts abrupt changes and triggers distractions in the business growth in the companies. Chaos in market occurs as innovation and technology breakthroughs are akin to the lifecycle of many industrial and consumer products comprising stages of introduction, acceleration (growth), acceptance (maturity), and renewal/diversification (decline). Each big idea catches hold slowly and moves through various stages from ideation to commercialization in the market, but chaos occurs in the market as many ideas grow in the market simultaneously. Yet, within a relatively short time, the new approach becomes so widely accepted that it is difficult even for old-timers to reconstruct how the world looked before. As the market competition is growing and consumers are rapidly shifting their preferences, most companies are moving to the verge of creative destruction, as survival options in the market have been narrowed down to philosophy of adapt, evolve, or perish. Accordingly, most companies are leaning toward continuous innovations to differentiate their products and services, but at the same time, they are also susceptible to failures due to random and non-tested efforts. Thus, the business in modern times poses uncertainty and moves along the routinized business strategies in a predetermined niche with common rationale of no pain, no gain. To understand the changing market and consumer behavior, the creative destruction may be necessary, and even preferable, in certain situations (Abrahamson 2004).

The community creation model in managing new businesses across the diverse market segments is a governance mechanism for managing innovation that lies between the hierarchy-based (closed) mechanism and the market-based (open) systems for new product management and driving butterfly effect. The community-centric model shifts the focus of innovation and drives the change process beyond the boundaries of the firm, to a community of individuals and firms that collaborate to create joint intellectual property. Such strategies involve community in spanning the change instituted by the company, setting ground rules for participation, and developing sustainable consumer behavior with differentiation. The community of creation model allows innovation-led changes to initially pass through a complex environment by striking a balance between order and chaos in the market (Sawhney and Prandelli 2000).

With the high advancement of information technology and business forecasting tools, most companies are able to sustain the short-run market chaos by predicting the future market dynamics. Most companies are also able to determine and interpret the competitor signals in the chaotic markets. The foreseen uncertainty due to chaos in the market is characterized by radical marketing elements comprising market communications. This causes loose ends for free interpretations, marginal differences with existing and substitute products, and varied use values. To manage market uncertainty and chaos, companies need to play pro-customer roles, drive loyalty toward corporate brands, and build confidence in the changing technology-led lifestyles to gain strategic competitive advantages. Companies must learn to ascertain the selection of the best mix of tools and techniques while driving changes though the differentiation in products and services and managing the market in chaos (Meyer et al. 2002).

Managing chaos in the market needs to be learned through the constructive strategies and analyzing multiple perspectives that have no fear of tarnishing the image of the company that is engaged in driving change in consumer behavior. In a growing market chaos among the several competitive products that have marginal differentiation, global organizations need to quickly develop the customer values to streamline the desired change in market and consumer attitudes. Large organizations, if led well, can do more for more people and flip the chaos, complexity, and pressure to manage the new market endeavors. *Nissan* Automobiles has been able to cope with crises among the Asian automobiles and chaos of low-cost cars, penetrating the potential emerging markets like India and China. The chaos was triggered by the *Nano* brand of Tata Motors Corporation in India, which promised low-end price in the mass market. Similarly, *Faw* Automobiles in China has driven its low-priced cars to the global markets. However, Nissan tried to cut through the chaos by generating diverse values concerning the quality and services among the consumers in the global markets (Barton et al. 2012).

Continuous market evolution across regions, products, and services had driven rapid diffusion of new products in the marketplace. Shorter time to market and shorter product lifecycles are pushing companies to introduce new products more frequently in the global marketplace. While new products intend to offer high value, product introductions and transitions pose enormous challenges to managers. Drawing from research at Intel, and examples from General Motors and Cisco Systems, it may be argued that the risks impacting a transition identify a set of factors across departments tracking those risks, monitor the evolution of these factors over time, and develop playbook mapping scenarios of risks and responses in the market. This process of market evolution nurturing the demand for new product helps firm's expectations in the marketplace, lowers the chance and impact of unanticipated outcomes, and helps synchronize the responses among different consumer segments (Erhun et al. 2007).

Cannibalization in Global Marketplace

Conceptually, in a chaotic marketplace, firms cannibalize when the products of a large firm compete for the same customers. However, customer defection, price wars, and deceptive communications also constitute the process of cannibalization. This becomes possible whenever a firm offers multiple products at low-end markets that are identical (e.g. purified bottled water) or somewhat similar (e.g. beverages with marginal differentiation in price, taste, and perceived value) to one another. Intense competition between firms in a particular segment (e.g. mobile phones), then products in that segment are more likely to cannibalize products from less competitive segments (e.g. laptops, and tablets). Cannibalization may also occur as a firm runs two parallel business models such as e-commerce and brick-and-mortar retailing operation. The business model providing digital sales at relatively low price to consumer as compared to brick-and-mortar stores due to higher overhead costs would cannibalize the market share across the channels within the company (Bordley and Karnani 2018).

The increasing competition in the global marketplace has induced large companies with high market share and brand equity to expand spatially their market operations. In this process, large companies tend to acquire smaller firms or get them merged with larger organizations on win–win negotiations. Although such process has been established in the global marketplace as an effective strategy for the growth of business for the larger companies, it has been considered as a survival for smaller and weaker companies in the market. In the context of global competition, this approach may be considered as a process of cannibalization. At the lower end of the market, value-added resellers (VAR) also catalyze the cannibalization in the global market. Remanufactured products do not always cannibalize new product sales. To minimize cannibalization and create additional profits, firms need to understand how consumers value remanufactured products. This is not a static decision and should be re-evaluated over the entire product lifecycle. While firms exhibit responsibility to maximize profits for the firm, this is not necessarily equivalent to maximizing new product sales. A portfolio that includes remanufactured products can enable firms to reach additional market segments and help them block competition from new low-end products or third-party remanufacturers (Atasu et al. 2010). The causes and effects of cannibalization in a competitive marketplace are exhibited in Figure 1.3.

Cannibalization in the market occurs due to the micro- and macro-marketing policies, as illustrated in Figure 1.3. Frequent introduction of low-end products (influx) with low prices stimulates market chaos. Companies in a chaotic marketplace tend to cannibalize the brands of competitors to gain minimum viable market share to survive the competition. However, low-cost market economics, disruptive innovations, and perceived value of consumer toward high-promotion and low-price products support the market chaos and increase the consumer surplus. Disruptive innovations also contribute to the market chaos and drive companies to take aggressive marketing decisions, which leads to

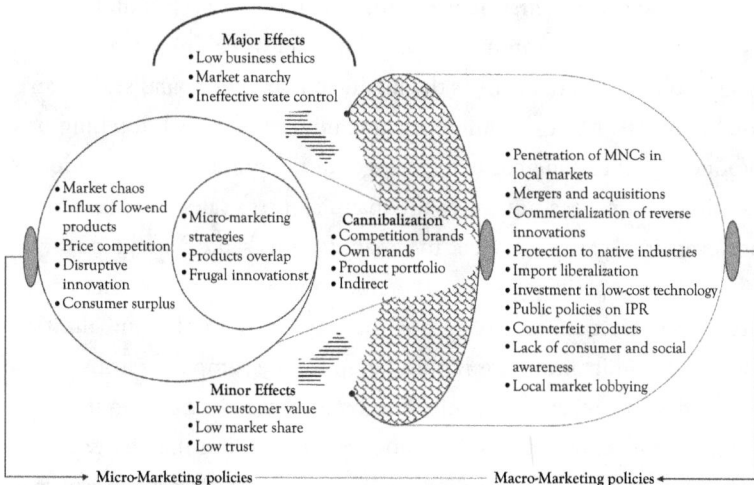

Figure 1.3 Ecosystem of cannibalization in the marketplace

Source: Author

cannibalization. Micromarketing strategies of a company grow out of the corporate decision on management of product-mix and marketing-mix. Most companies follow the product overlap strategy to increase the length of the product line within a product portfolio by introducing products with marginal differentiation in attributes, prescribed use value, and end-user price. Such overlapping of products in a product line instigates cannibalization of brands within the product line of the same company to augment brand-specific market share. Fugal innovations also aggravate cannibalization within the company. The major effects of cannibalization exhibit lack of business ethics among the market players, unregulated marketing practices causing anarchy in the marketplace, and fall into ineffective state control in market operations. Figure 1.3 also illustrates the macro-marketing factors that cause cannibalization of brands in the competitive marketplace. Besides aggressive penetration of products and services of multinational companies in the local markets, market chaos causes mergers and acquisitions, commercialization of reverse innovations (low-cost innovative products by multinational companies), public policies on protection of native companies, low control on intellectual property rights, rise of counterfeit products, and lack of consumer and social awareness on chaotic products.

In a global competitive marketplace, a large manufacturer may sell new products in the first quarter of the financial year (FY) and face the threat of cannibalization in the second quarter of FY from a competitor, which collects and refurbishes the manufacturer's goods and sells them as used products. Most e-commerce companies are engaged in selling used products after making cosmetic changes in the products. In this process, cannibalization does not lower the manufacturer's sales in both periods; however, it negatively affects the manufacturer's profits and positively affects the competitor's profits. Therefore, a reduction in the price of new products is never enough to counter the negative effect of cannibalization. However, cannibalization is harmful even for the competing firms, whose profits decrease when the cannibalization level exceeds a certain threshold (Ramani and Giovanni 2017). Thus, cannibalization may be explained as a business situation and lifecycle like any other element in the marketing-mix. Most companies have switched to multichannel operational model. Among the multichannel operations, Internet channels account for nearly half of the total channels, which potentially cannibalize the market share of brick-and-mortar channels. Internet channels augment the performance of sales of companies in existing markets and help them enter new markets (Sharma et al. 2018). However, Internet channels increase ambiguity in market adherence, create real-time risks, and jeopardize the returns on capital invested by the companies toward building marketing and sales infrastructure. Internet-based retailing is growing fast in emerging markets and attracting a significant proportion of customers by providing convenience of buying and better customer services than the brick-and-mortar stores. The defection of consumers across the channels is identified as virtual cannibalization of the own channels of a firm as well as of competitors (Thaichon et al. 2018).

Firms in the competitive marketplace should analyze the effects of price and non-price promotional incentives on market shares of brands within a product category to differentiate between cannibalization and competitive effects. The question is to what extent the growth in market share derived from a promotion comes at the expense of other product sizes of the same brand within the category (cannibalization) or at the expense of the other brands within the category (competition). Cannibalization in global marketplace is very common in the liberal entry policies adopted by many countries in response to globalization. Expansion of product lines and continuous innovations drive cannibalization not only for the competing products, but also within the product line of a company. Companies often design product lines by segmenting their markets on quality attributes that exhibit a *more is better* or *value for money* property for all consumers. Products within a product line with marginal differentiation, which compete as close substitutes, often create competition among themselves. Multiproduct firms need to meticulously address the cannibalization problem in designing their product lines and avoid product overlaps. It has been observed that if lower-quality products are attractive, consumers having concern for *value for money* may find it beneficial to buy lower-quality products rather than the higher-quality products targeted to them. Accordingly, lower-quality products can potentially cannibalize higher-quality products. The cannibalization problem forces the firm to provide only the highest-valuation segment with its preferred quality, while other segments get qualities lower than anticipated.

The firm may not serve some of the lowest-valuation segments when the cannibalization problem is very severe. However, not much is known about how and when the cannibalization problem affects the product line design in an oligopoly. In addition, consumers may differ not only in their quality valuations, but also in their taste preferences (Desai 2001).

In centralized firms, with limited product portfolios and short product line, appropriately altering the design and pricing of different products could manage cannibalization. However, decentralized firms with autonomy across the manufacturing and marketing division struggle to lead the market within the group of companies (umbrella corporate structure). A decentralized corporate structure like General Electric Company differentiates their manufacturing and marketing systems so that each unit (department or division) grows in a different business ecosystem. Most decentralized firms have interdependencies in organizational resources, technology, and corporate brand management, which, in a passive way, develop strategic synergy, or in an aggressive manner, drive cannibalization behavior across their business divisions. Successful, large, multi-division companies manage these interdependencies in context of the overall corporate environment (Boardly and Karnan 2018). General Motors (GM) is also globally identified as a good example of a multi-divisional organization. The price segmentation discouraged cannibalization across the automobile divisions manufacturing different brands of automobile, while the centralized profit-sharing policy of the company streamlined the operational decision-making. Such strategy was defined as coordinated decentralization (Birkinshaw and Lingblad 2005).

Under some conditions, the cannibalization problem does not affect the firms' price and quality choices, and each firm provides each segment with that segment's preferred quality. Each firm finds it optimal to serve both segments. In case the consumer preferences of the high-valuation segments are sufficiently weak, more intense competition in the high-valuation segment is expected to reduce that segment's incentives to buy the product meant for the low-valuation segment. This mitigates the cannibalization problem and makes it more likely for the low-valuation segment to get its preferred quality. Similarly, when firms are less differentiated in the low-valuation segment, stronger competition between the firms makes the cannibalization problem worse, and the low-valuation segment may not get its preferred quality (Desai 2001). Cannibalization has also become a critical phenomenon in selling products and services of identical nature in the competitive consumer segment. Consider a seller who faces two customer segments with differing valuations of quality of a durable product where demand is stationary and known, the technology exists to release two products simultaneously, and the seller can commit in advance to subsequent prices and qualities. Should the seller introduce two differentiated products simultaneously? Under the simultaneous strategy, the lower quality would cannibalize demand for the higher quality. To reduce cannibalization, the seller could lower the quality of the low-end model and reduce the price of the high-end model. Alternatively, he or she could increase the quality of the low-end model, but delay its release (Moorthy and Png 1992).

Multichannel marketing strategies encourage cannibalization of intra- and inter-company brands of consumer product. Channel conflicts in multichannel systems often occur, as companies tend to attract consumers by various promotions on marketing-mix elements, which potentially leads to the cannibalization of sales across the channels. The possibility of cannibalization of brands in multichannel marketing increases because of faster outreach of consumer experiences on social media. In addition, common sales infrastructure, common operations, and common marketing strategies across the brands in markets encourage the incidence of cannibalization of brands (Kollmann et al. 2012). Firms cannibalize in the marketplace to seize market share of competing firms using different approaches. Large firms adopt long-terms plans as competitive strategies, while small firms follow tactical and myopic approaches to gain higher market share in short span surpassing the existing firms. The common attributes of cannibalization include:

- Use of disruptive technology
- Engaging in price war
- Introduction of new products
- Developing extensive customer loyalty programs
- Improving customer services
- Enhancing the quality
- Augmenting the value for money

Firms that have innovative strategies also exhibit the cannibalization attributes. The success of such attackers in gaining market share has created a big dilemma for established companies. By embracing the new business models introduced by the innovators in the markets, established companies can potentially take advantage of a great growth opportunity. The new business models often conflict with the established ones. It has been observed that the challenge for companies is to balance the benefits of keeping the new and existing business models separate while integrating them enough to allow them to exploit synergies with one another (Markides and Charitou 2004).

Taxonomy of Market Competition

In the context of Darwinian fitness, market competition in the local markets tends to be oligopolistic with low-end products as frugal innovation increases. Multinational companies also differentiate the brands and develop price competitive business plans to cater to the markets in developing economies. The price competitive business model of large companies serves as an effective strategy in local markets on the one hand, and tends to explore the possibilities of a merger and acquisition (M&A) of local firms on the other. The chaotic growth of low-price competition is controlled through M&A strategies at the bottom of the pyramid, which benefits large companies with the near monopolistic market attributes. When local business dynamics is regained over time, the relationship between competition and innovation appears to be richer than before in local markets. Large companies, which enjoy niche business after successful M&A of local companies, face oligopolistic competition in the long term, as the local competitors stimulate the market again with frugal innovations. The cycle of near-monopoly to oligopolistic market competition continues in the local marketplace.

Oligopolistic markets compete on price, and chaos in the market is caused by the degree of substitution between the products, services, experimental consumer behavior, and awareness among consumers on the new brands. The social media and business information services generally play critical role in instigating chaotic behavior among consumers. Therefore, in competitive markets, an innovation is driven by the *escape competition* effect, which explains the difference between the payoffs before and after the introduction of frugal innovations or vogue brands by competing companies in the marketplace. However, markets that are engaged in the high-technology and high-value products are able to control the competition with few market players and increase industry's pace of innovation and consumer surplus in the long term (Marshall and Parra 2019). Consumer surplus can be explained as the difference between the price that consumers pay and the price that they are willing to pay. In a broader sense, this phenomenon may also be synthesized as perceived value for money.

In an oligopolistic market competition, there are only a few firms that make up an industry. This select group of firms has control over the price and, like a monopoly, an oligopoly has high barriers to entry. The products that the oligopolistic firms produce are often nearly identical, and the companies, which are competing for market share, are interdependent as a result of market forces. The fostering of successful private companies becomes particularly attractive in global markets. The clearest example is the Internet, in which China's state-controlled news providers and broadcasters have the resources and content to succeed, but have failed to create much noise. There is no single theory of how firms determine price and output under conditions of oligopoly. An oligopolistic market usually exhibits the following features:

- Product branding: Each firm in the market is selling a branded (differentiated) product.
- Entry barriers: Significant entry barriers into the market prevent the dilution of competition in the long term, which maintains supernormal profits for the dominant firms. It is perfectly possible for many smaller firms to operate on the periphery of an oligopolistic market, but none of them is large enough to have any significant effect on market prices and output.
- Interdependent decision-making: Interdependence means that firms must consider the possible reactions of their rivals to any change in price, output, or forms of non-price competition. In perfect competition and monopoly, the producers do

not have to consider a rival's response when choosing output and price.

- Non-price competition: Non-price competition is a consistent feature of the competitive strategies of oligopolistic firms. Examples of non-price competition include:
  - Free deliveries and installation
  - Extended warranties for consumers and credit facilities
  - Longer opening hours (e.g., supermarkets and petrol stations)
  - Branding of products and heavy spending on advertising and marketing
  - Extensive after-sales service
  - Expanding into new markets and diversification of the product range

Oligopoly is considered as a healthy ambience for market competition. In this pattern of competition, market leaders need challengers to keep them dynamic in the marketplace. For example, consider Microsoft Corporation's curious love–hate tango with Netscape Communications Corporation. In the ongoing government antitrust trial, Microsoft faces allegations that it first proposed dividing the Internet browser market with Netscape, creating a nice little oligopoly for the two of them, and then attempted to crush the fledgling company when it refused. Microsoft denies that occurred. Still, it is clear that Netscape's existence prodded Microsoft to pour huge resources into improving its own browser (Zachary 1999).

Some markets like that of green energy industry, with exclusivity of combinations of products and services, exhibit some form of imperfect or monopolistic competition. There are fewer firms than in a perfectly competitive market, and each can create barriers to entry to some degree. A firm may own a crucial resource such as an oil well, or power generator, or it may have an exclusive operating license, which restricts other competitors from entering the business. Operating on economies of scale for a large firm may also have a significant competitive advantage, as it may enjoy a large volume of production at lower cost, which may further lead to the price leadership with low retail prices. Such strategy would also prevent the potential competitors from entering in the business. An incumbent firm may make it hard for a would-be entrant by incurring huge sunk costs with high budget advertising. In view of such strategy, any new entrant may match to compete effectively, but may lose the market share if the attempt to compete fails. Sunk costs are the costs that have been incurred and cannot be reversed such as spending on advertising or researching a product idea. They can be barriers to entry. If potential entrants have to incur similar costs, which would not be recoverable if the entry failed, they may be scared off. Another radical strategy may be used by powerful firms to discourage entry by raising exit costs, for example, by making it an industry norm to hire workers on long-term contracts, which would build the escalated cost barriers for rival companies. Thus, firms can earn some excess profits without a new entrant being able to compete to bring prices down.

The monopolistic market today has developed in the categorical industrial sectors such as public media in socialist countries, petroleum industry in developing economies, and defense equipment manufacturing industry, which are operated as state-controlled industries. The market barriers in these industries are legal and regulatory within the economic and political limitations. Technology is another area of industrial monopoly like iOS operating system or mobile devices. iOS is a mobile operating system created and developed by Apple Inc. exclusively for its hardware. It also powered the iPad prior to the introduction of iPad OS in 2019. Technology development and marketing are integrated in the contemporary model of monopolistic competition that analyzes the structural effects on demand and changes in the market size. Companies serving mass-consumer segments in local and international markets tend to adapt to technologies that support economics of scale operations. If a technology switch occurs due to the development of new generations, firms that are short of resources to meet its costs withdraw from manufacturing and marketing the technology-led products. Consequently, a rationalizing effect arises within the industry individual, and the aggregate output increases, resulting into fall in prices. However, this development need not benefit consumers because a technology switch is associated with a decrease in product-mix comprising product portfolios and length (Elberfeld and Götz 2002).

Monopolistic competition in the marketplace holds the control of a single firm over its products and influences the market price of its product by altering the rate of production. Monopolistic firms are engaged with such products that are not perfect substitutes or are at least perceived to be different from all other brands products. Unlike in perfect competition, the monopolistic firm does not produce at the lowest possible average total cost. Instead, the firm produces at an inefficient output level, reaping more in additional revenue than it incurs in additional cost versus the efficient output level. Such firms produce identical products, except for branding, but due to a relatively low number of firms, which control the vast amount of the products, can control the price to an extent by decreasing supply slightly. Contrary to the monopolistic firms in the market, there exists perfect competition. Perfect competition is an economic model that describes a hypothetical market in which no producer or consumer has the market power to influence prices. While monopolistic competition is inefficient, perfect competition is the most efficient, with supply meeting demand and matching with the production incurring minimal or no costs on inventory. However, there exists a near-monopoly market of coal sector in India. Coal is abundant in the country and is largely used in the production of thermal power. As the country is moving toward globalization, the demand for thermal electricity will continue to rise, roughly in line with economic growth. India has the world's fifth-largest coal reserves (*The Economist* 2012).

The contemporary ideology on competition emphasizes largely on the competitive environment, which contributes to various dimensions of rivalries. It has been observed that the low-end competitor indulging a company in offering much lower prices for a seemingly similar product has been the common fear of each industry leader managing its business among competitors. The vast majority of such low-end companies falls into one of the four broad categories, which include strippers, predators, reformers, or transformers (Potter 2004). Each of these is defined by the functionality of product and the convenience of purchase. Industry leaders have significant advantages to combat low-end competition following low-price and high-value strategy, but they often hesitate, as their actions might adversely affect the market share and current profit. The solution, then, may be to find the response that is most likely to restore market calm in the least disruptive way. An industry leader could choose to ride out the challenge by ignoring, blocking, or acquiring the low-end competitor, or it could decide to strengthen its own value proposition by adding new price points, increasing its level of benefits, or dropping its prices. Such tactics can be effective in the short term, but the industry leader also needs to consider strategic retreat, particularly when certain conditions make future low-end challenges inevitable.

Competitor Learning

There are many ways of competitor learning process. Comparative learning occurs when two or more competitors are compared and contrasted. It especially entails analysis of outputs, which is necessary frequently to compare and contrast the projections of two or more competitors' future strategies as a means of anticipating which competitors are likely to do what and when. It is also often necessary to compare and contrast how competitors are responding to the focal firm's own initiatives. The process of descriptive learning of competitors involves learning about the individual competitors at the basic level in reference to capturing the processing data and information about the competitor to identify the facts and features. This learning tool supports the inputs to comparative learning. Many of the concepts and analysis tools such as marketplace strategic activity, value chain, assumptions, resources, and competency facilitate comparisons across two or more competitors. The comparative learning process generates insights and inferences that cannot be derived by examining individual competitors in isolation. Learning is a cognitive process as customer decisions make sense of the world around them. They select and array the information, permeate data with meaning, draw inferences from incomplete data, and portray the results. Learning is also a collective process, though transforming individual learning into organizational learning is a difficult task. Learning truly occurs when individuals share their knowledge, challenge each other, and reflect on each other's judgments and assessments.

Collecting information on competitor philosophy, strategies, and moves need to be further clustered (in case of homogeneity) or fragmented (in case of heterogeneity) to understand the micro- and macro contents. Commonly, competition information needs to be fragmented and analyzed to learn about competitor strategy. It is very similar to the second law of thermodynamics, which states that the total entropy of an isolated system can never decrease over time. The total entropy of a system and its surroundings can remain constant in ideal cases where the system is in thermodynamic equilibrium. This principle applies also to market equilibrium in the context of competition—monopolistic or oligopolistic. Emerging research studies propose to measure the hidden (entropy) costs of inventory systems in context of the second law of thermodynamics, while another stream of research focuses on learning by doing, which reduces the unit cost of a product causing reduction in the prices of products and services, and enhancing the competitiveness of the firm (Jaber et al. 2019).

The two core concepts of the competitor learning process are *efficient learning* and *effective learning*. The former refers to the learning input–output ratio. The input for the learning process is the competitor data, and the output includes the change in knowledge level. The effective competitor learning addresses the output–decision relationship. In the process of competitor learning, both efficiency and effectiveness need attention and require data, information, and intelligence. Data constitutes the basic input in the process of competitor learning. The data about any competitor may be put into three broad categories, namely behavioral pattern of the competitor, statements pertaining to the competitor, and organization change. The individual actions of competitors or the patterns displayed thereof are referred as the competitor behavior. The actions may be analyzed in reference to the marketplace strategy, customer relationship, brand management, sales and promotion of the products and services in the region. The statements of the competitors may be of various types such as the performance data, announcements, annual reports and the like.

It is necessary to look into some of the information errors that may occur during the data collection process. The fallacy of misplaced facts is the most common problem in data collection. The information on the projections of the cash flows, sales, and production levels is more vulnerable for the competitors, customers, and investors. The information error also constitutes the misconstrued pattern or underlying structure in a set of information or data. Such information errors are based on the assumptions drawn by the information collectors and disseminators. However, the exaggerated information provided to the strategy builder or decision makers is also one of the common information errors that occur in the process of outwitting the competitor from the market. Evidence for the success of relationship marketing remains contradictory, with practitioners reporting that most relationship marketing efforts fail, and academic researchers suggesting that further exploration of the boundary conditions of relationship marketing is needed. A number of researchers have identified changes in the competitive environment as the basis for the adoption of relationship marketing, although recent research suggests a more complex, contingent view (Beverland and Lindgreen 2004).

A common mistake many firms make is to start by collecting information without thinking how the information will be used. Such junk data has no value, and it is just shelved. The information needs to be comprehensive and adequate to help analysis of the strategic or tactical decisions on the role of competitors using vital business indicators. If a firm is planning to launch a new product, information on the status of the competitors in the area will help in the decision processes and plans for this new product. Alternatively, the firm may review how the industry will develop in future toward the market leadership, potential merger, and acquisition or business partnership. The information requirements for each of these business decisions will be completely different; therefore, the information that should be sought will also be different. Thus, before starting to search for information, the competitor analyst needs to sit back and define what the firm is looking for and why. It is important to identify the key areas of concern for the business decision makers requesting the information and aim to satisfy these areas. The supplementary information may be interesting; but unless it helps the decision process, it should be viewed as superfluous and stored for use at another time or even ignored if it is unlikely to ever have value. Hence, a firm may streamline its search needs toward better planned and focused strategies, which would help in answering various intelligence requirements of the business.

It is essential that any company planning for competitive strategies should possess high learning skills to collect right information, analyze it, and interpret the results. The organization's knowledge about the competitor and its moves broadly consists of perceptions, beliefs, assumptions, and projections. Learning as the detection and correction process has varied implications for outwitting, outmaneuvering, and outperforming the competitors. Single-loop learning may occur when the organization detects and corrects the knowledge base without changing thrust on its strategies and actions. This is a closed and confined learning method that does not allow reviewing or re-engineering the information spool. On the contrary, in the double-loop learning process, the organizational knowledge, information base, and strategies, in addition to its action plans, are open for review and re-engineering in the long-term interest of the company.

There are three levels of competitor analysis—a system, an individual competitor, and the specific components of the competitor. The framework of competitor analysis includes the infrastructure and culture of an organization and value chain, networks, and relationships representing the environment of the company. The entire analysis must focus on the current strategy of the competitor firm and its future steps. Besides the assumptions in business risks and prospects, it is also important to analyze the assets, capabilities, competence levels, and technology usage of the competing firm. In all these exercises, the data must be reliable and comprehensive to make the competitor learning process stronger. Signals are perhaps the most important core concepts in competitor learning. A signal is an inference drawn by an individual in some specific context from the data and information about a competitor pertaining to the past, current, and future strategies. The core components of the signal are indicators of the data and information. The inferences drawn on signals received from the competitors based on data enable deriving the strategies for implementation.

A competitor signal is difficult to interpret and assess if there is no proper database and the indicators are not relevant. The ambiguity about indicators may occur by words, actions, unclear strategies of the organization, and biased information. The signals from the competitor may be direct or indirect. The analyst needs logical aptitude and strong reasoning to use the indirect signals appropriately for building strategies. The competitors send signals in the market about all the vital indicators of business such as products, services, advertisement, prices, channels, and so on in a distorted fashion to weaken the business rivals. Therefore, it is necessary to capture the signals well in time and draw inferences. Late attention to the signals may lead to detection lag caused due to the extended length of time between the availability of the information and its capture by the analyst. Competitors' signaling is very volatile and needs to be attended immediately to avoid any time lag or delay in drawing the inferences out of the available information.

Competitive intelligence also contributes to the learning process of a growing firm. Competitive intelligence is the information available to the competitors for free access on the public resources, which is periodically updated to present the current contents and potential strategic information. The information acquired by the competitors through public sources serves as an important input in formulating their marketing strategy. A firm must be aware of the perspectives of its competitors before deciding which competitive moves to make. Competitive intelligence includes information beyond industry statistics and trade gossip. It involves close observation of the competitors to learn what they do best and why and where they are weak. There are three types of competitive intelligence—defensive, passive, and offensive. Defensive intelligence is the information gathered, analyzed, and used to avoid being caught off-balance. In this process, a deliberate attempt is made by the competing firm to gather information on the prevailing competition in a structured fashion and to keep track of moves of the rivals that are relevant to the firm's business. Passive intelligence is the temporary information gathered for a specific decision. A company may, for example, seek information on a competitor's sales compensation plan when devising its own compensation plan. Offensive intelligence is the information gathered by the firms to identify new opportunities and from a strategic perspective; such intelligence is most relevant for a growing firm amidst competition.

Summary

Darwinian fitness, in the context of business, reveals the phenomenon of continuous evolution of firms within vertical and horizontal market competition. Vertical expansion of business firms occurs when they widen tine product-mix across the product portfolios and increase the length of product line within the portfolios within a predetermined market, while horizontal expansion of business is found across geo-demographic segments and destinations. Darwinian fitness in business explains metaphorically the two principles of evolution—survival of the fittest (multinational companies in the bottom-of-the-pyramid market segments) and struggle for existence (local firms aiming to break the niche and go global). Such downward and upward strategic moves of companies in business cause 3Cs comprising chaos, crisis, and complexity in behavior of market players, including consumers. Chaotic behavior is nonlinear and fuzzy, which is unable to predict. However, in some controlled situations, chaotic market behavior is predictable for a while and then appears to become random, driving consumers in a dilemma to respond to the uncertain marketing strategies of the companies. Discussions in this chapter discuss the causes and effects of chaos in market.

Chaotic behavior in business induces companies to cannibalize competing products and services, which conforms to both principles of Darwinism—survival of the fittest and struggle for existence. Therefore, cannibalization is considered as an effect of market chaos caused due to high competition among identical and similar products. Often, overlapping products within a product portfolio cannibalize each other to gain market share. Discussions in the chapter reveal that cannibalization is a complex business situation and has a lifecycle. Most companies have switched to the multichannel operational model, which is more susceptible to cannibalization within the product-mix of a company. Cannibalization in the global marketplace is very common in the liberal entry policies adopted by many countries in response to globalization. It has also become a critical phenomenon in selling products and services of identical nature in the competitive consumer segment.

Oligopolistic markets, both at the high and low end, trigger chaos in market. Price is one of major determinant of market chaos alongside of frugal innovation at the low-end markets. The price competitiveness drives substitution among the products, services, experimental consumer behavior, and awareness among consumers on the new brands. The monopolistic market does not exist today in a broad sense, but near-monopoly is a situation that occurs with the market leader companies for a limited period until competition emerges from the local or global ends.

This chapter addresses these intricacies of market competition. It is argued that one of the good ways to understand market complexity caused due to the various attributes of competition and its taxonomy is a systematic learning of competitors' signals and strategies. Learning is a cognitive process by understanding of array the information, infusing data with right interpretations, and drawing inferences. Commonly, competition information needs to be fragmented and analyzed to learn about competitor strategy.

References

Abrahamson, E. 2004. "Avoiding Repetitive Change Syndrome." *Sloan Management Review* 45, no. 2, pp. 93–95.

Atasu, A., V.D.R. Guide, Jr, and L.N.V. Wassenhove. 2010. "So What If Remanufacturing Cannibalizes My New Product Sales?" *California Management Review* 52, no. 2, pp. 56–76.

Barton, D., A. Grant, and M. Horn. 2012. "Leading in the Twenty First Century." *McKinsey Quarterly.*

Beverland, M., and A. Lindgreen. 2004. "Relationship Use and Market Dynamism-A Model of Relationship Evolution." *Journal of Marketing Management* 20, no. 7–8, pp. 825–58.

Birkinshaw, J., and M. Lingblad. 2005. "Intrafirm Competition and Charter Evolution in the Multibusiness Firm." *Organization Science* 16, no. 6, pp. 674–86.

Bordley, R.F., and A. Karnani. 2018. "Using Incentives to Address Cannibalization." *Long Range Planning* 51, no. 5, pp. 641–48.

Brown, S.L., and K.M. Eisenhardt. 1998. *Competing on the Edge.* Boston, MA: Harvard Business School Press.

Cowling, M., W. Liu, and A. Ledger. 2015. "What Really Happens to Small and Medium-Sized Enterprises in a Global Economic Recession? UK Evidence on Sales and Job Dynamics." *International Small Business Journal* 33, no. 5, pp. 488–513.

Debruyne, M., and D.J. Reibstein. 2005. "Competitor See, Competitor Do: Incumbent Entry in New Market Niches." *Marketing Science* 24, no. 1, pp. 55–66.

Desai, P.S. 2001. "Quality Segmentation in Spatial Markets: When Does Cannibalization Affect Product Line Design?" *Marketing Science* 20, no. 3, pp. 265–83.

Desmet, K., and S.L. Parente. 2010. "Bigger Is Better: Market Size, Demand Elasticity, and Innovation." *International Economic Review* 51, no. 2, pp. 319–33.

Elberfeld, W., and G. Götz. 2002. "Market Size, Technology Choice, and Market Structure." *German Economic Review* 3, no. 1, pp. 25–41.

Erhun, F., P. Concalves, and J. Hopman. 2007. "Art of Managing New Products Transition." *MIT Sloan Management Review* 48, no. 3, pp. 73–80.

Espínola-Arredondo, A., E. Gal-Or, and F. Muñoz-García. 2011. "When Should a Firm Expand Its Business? The Signaling Implications of Business Expansion." *International Journal of Industrial Organization* 29, no. 6, pp. 729–45.

Giaglis, G.M., and K.G. Fouskas. 2011. "The Impact of Managerial Perceptions on Competitive Response Variety." *Management Decision* 49, no. 8, pp. 1257–75.

Goldthorpe, J.H. 2000a. "Globalisation and Social Class." *West European Politics* 25, no. 3, pp. 1–28.

Harrison, R.L., III, K.D. Thomas, and S.N.N. Cross. 2017. "Restricted Visions of Multiracial Identity in Advertising." *Journal of Advertising* 46, no. 4, pp. 503–20.

Hedaa, L., and T. Ritter. 2005. "Business Relationships on Different Waves: Paradigm Shift and Marketing Orientation Revisited." *Industrial Marketing Management* 34, no. 7, pp. 714–21.

Houry, S.A. 2012. "Chaos and Organizational Emergence: Towards Short Term Predictive Modeling to Navigate a Way Out of Chaos." *Systems Engineering Procedia* 3, pp. 229–39.

Huneman, P. 2019. "Revisiting Darwinian Teleology: A Case for Inclusive Fitness as Design Explanation." *Studies in History and Philosophy of Science Part C. Studies in History and Philosophy of Biological and Biomedical Sciences* 76, Art 101188.

Jaber, M.Y., B. Marchi, and S. Zanoni. 2019. "Learning-by-Doing May Not Be Enough to Sustain Competitiveness in a Market." *Applied Mathematical Modelling* 75, pp. 627–39.

Klioutchnikov, I., M. Sigova, and N. Beizerov. 2017. "Chaos Theory in Finance." *Procedia Computer Science* 119, pp. 368–75.

Kollmann, T., A. Kuckertz, and I. Kayser. 2012. "Cannibalization or Synergy? Consumers' Channel Selection in Online-Offline Multichannel Systems." *Journal of Retailing and Consumer Services* 19, no. 2, pp. 186–94.

Lawler, E.K., A. Hedge, and S. Pavlovic-Veselinovic. 2011. "Cognitive Ergonomics, Socio-Technical Systems, and the Impact of Healthcare Information Technologies." *International Journal of Industrial Ergonomics* 41, no. 4, pp. 336–44.

Licsandru, T.C., and C.C. Cui. 2019. "Ethnic Marketing to the Global Millennial Consumers: Challenges and Opportunities." *Journal of Business Research* 103, pp. 261–74.

Li, Y., and L. Wang. 2019. "Chaos in a Duopoly Model of Technological Innovation with Bounded Rationality Based on Constant Conjectural Variation." *Chaos, Solitons & Fractals* 120, pp. 116–26.

Markides, C., and C.D. Charitou. 2004. "Competing with Dual Business Models: A Contingency Approach." *The Academy of Management Executive* 18, no. 3, pp. 22–36.

Marshall, G., and A. Parra. 2019. "Innovation and Competition: The Role of the Product Market." *International Journal of Industrial Organization* 65, no. 2, pp. 221–47.

Meyer, A.D., C.H. Loch, and M.T. Pich. 2002. *Sloan Management Review* 43, no. 2, pp. 60–67.

Moorthy, K.S., and I.P.L. Png. 1992. "Market Segmentation, Cannibalization, and the Timing of Product Introductions." *Management Science* 38, no. 3, pp. 345–59.

Mossio, M., C. Saborido, and A. Moreno. 2009. "An Organizational Account of Biological Functions." *The British Journal for the Philosophy of Science* 60, pp. 813–41.

Potter, D. 2004. "Confronting Low-End Competition." *Sloan Management Review* 45, no. 4, pp. 73–79.

Quinn, J.B. 1985. "Managing Innovation: Controlled Chaos." *Harvard Business Review* 63, no. 3, pp. 73–84.

Rajagopal. 2012. *Darwinian Fitness in the Global Marketplace: Analyzing the Competition.* Basingstoke, UK: Palgrave Macmillan.

Rajagopal. 2015. *Butterfly Effect in Competitive Markets: Driving Small Change for Larger Differences.* Basingstoke, UK: Palgrave Macmillan.

Rajagopal. 2016. *Innovative Business Projects: Breaking Complexities, Building Performance (Vol.2)-Financials, New Insights, and Project Sustainability.* New York, NY: Business Expert Press.

Ramani, V., and P.D. Giovanni. 2017. "A Two-Period Model of Product Cannibalization in an Atypical Closed-Loop Supply Chain with Endogenous Returns: The Case of DellReconnect." *European Journal of Operational Research* 262, no. 3, pp. 1009–27.

Sawhney, M., and E. Prandelli. 2000. "Communities of Creation: Managing Distributed Innovation in Turbulent Markets." *California Management Review* 42, no. 4, pp. 24–54.

Scott, J.A., and W.C. Dunkelberg. 2010. "Competition for Small Firm Banking Business: Bank Actions versus Market Structure." *Journal of Banking & Finance* 34, no. 11, pp. 2788–2800.

Shapiro, J. 2011. *Evolution: A View from the 21st Century*. San Francisco: FT Press Science.

Sharma, D., S.K. Pandey, R. Chandwani, P. Pandey, and R. Joseph. 2018. "Internet Channel Cannibalization and Its Influence on Salesperson Performance Outcomes in an Emerging Economy Context." *Journal of Retailing and Consumer Services* 45, no. 2, pp. 179–89.

Shih, C.C., T.M.Y. Lin, and P. Luarn. 2014. "Fan-Centric Social Media: The Xiaomi Phenomenon in China." *Business Horizons* 57, no. 3, pp. 349–58.

Strikwerda, J., and J.W. Stoelhorst. 2009. "The Emergence and Evolution of the Multidimensional Organizations." *California Management Review* 51, no. 4, pp. 11–31.

Thaichon, P., J. Surachartkumtonkun, S. Quach, S. Weaven, and R.W. Palmatier. 2018. "Hybrid Sales Structures in the Age of E-Commerce." *Journal of Personal Selling and Sales Management* 38, no. 3, pp. 277–302.

The Economist. 2012. "Future Is Black." In *The Economist*, January 21 Print edition.

Turner, S., and A. Endres. 2017. "Strategies for Enhancing Small-Business Owners' Success Rates." *International Journal of Advanced Manufacturing Technology* 16, no. 1, pp. 34–49.

Weick, R.D., and K.M. Sutcliffe. 2001. *Managing the Unexpected: Resilient Performance in an Age of Uncertainty*. San Francisco, CA: Jossey-Bass.

West, S.A., and A. Gardner. 2013. "Adaptation and Inclusive Fitness." *Current Biology* 23, pp. R557–R584.

Wheeler, M.A. 2004. *Turn Chaos to Your Advantage*. Boston, MA: Harvard Business School Publishing.

Zachary, G.P. 1999. "Many Industries Are Congealing into Lineup of Few Dominant Giants." *The Wall Street Journal*, p. B1.

CHAPTER 2
Contextual Market Entropy

Overview

Continuous shifts in consumer behavior and marketing strategies of companies cause fragmentation of large markets into niches and limit the scope of business growth. Growing market competition and chaos of identical and similar products often hinder the consumption behavior and corporate profitability in the long term. This chapter discusses the attributes of conventional markets, with a focus on complexities of niche markets and the changing retailing and shopping behavior of consumers. The effects of shifts in consumer behavior and consumption patterns from niche to the large markets have been discussed under the sub-section on simulated chaos. This chapter argues that shifts in the consumer behavior in niche markets drive rapid changes at a large scale across geo-demographic segments in the marketplace, which lead to the market fragmentation and market entropy in the long term. The causes and effects of demand fragmentation, consumer defection, and price entropy have also been discussed in this chapter.

Conventional Markets

Most conventional markets operate in niche and with limited geo-demographic segments, with more focus on customers than the competition. Traditional businesses relied on passive marketing under predetermined demand conditions in the market instead of going aggressive to create demand for their brands. These companies have widely followed demand-led marketing strategies and intended to serve the markets where demand existed. Such marketing behavior has saved their cost of marketing and uncertainty of gaining the market share. Companies operating on a low-risk business model have often compromised with low market share and marginality in profit. As the competition grows and consumer preferences often shift toward new market domains, mass markets fragment into several small niches. The market entropy is visible in mass markets, as they reorganize business operations into smaller market segments or niches due to market chaos and cannibalization. In minimum viable segments, companies feel safer from cut-throat competition and could explore new market opportunities. For many large companies aiming to penetrate remote destinations, fragmenting the market segments is considered a part of their positioning strategy for products and services. Niche marketing is often used as a deliberate marketing strategy to ensure business safety, increase customer value, and plan vertical expansion within the territorial limits (Dalgic and Leeuw 1994).

Niche Marketing Strategy

Multinational and large domestic firms offer standardized and mass-produced products that are adapted to the preferences of various geo-demographic segments. Such product portfolios cater to large supermarket chains, which serve mass-consumer segments. The local competitors also tend to manufacture their products to adapt to the needs of the niche markets, emphasizing the importance of destination brands, their identity, and contextual geo-demographic attributes to enhance product quality. The strategy of companies to create and manage niche markets is typically characterized by demand-led manufacturing, branding, and marketing to develop long-term customer relationships (Hammervoll 2014). Niche markets focus on small, profitable, and homogeneous market segments, which are also redefined as minimum viable market segments. Niche marketing strategy has outgrown as one of the popular conventional marketing designs. Niches or minimum viable segments in traditional market settings focus on a narrow share of the total market pie and operate on lower costs than the large companies. The niche markets operate within unique preferences and cater to the needs of a narrow, well-defined group of buyers, better than the potential rivals (Toften and Hammervoll 2013). However, over time, niche markets tend to face oligopolistic market competition, where each competitor operates in a niche of similar or identical product portfolios, causing further fragmentation of geo-demographic segments. Such business scenario, over a longer period, drives market entropy, which can be explained as a degenerating market phenomenon. Market entropy causes unregulated market competition, narrowing market segment, thin market shares among competitors, operational chaos, and asymmetric consumer defection across brands.

Niche strategies provide a classic instance of such situations. No market is entirely homogeneous. There are always groups of customers that differ in terms of their needs. The possibility of the occurrence of niches, which individual competitors may occupy, always exists. Niches are unlikely to be complete, separate, and well defined. There is always some overlap. However, if such niches are rather subtly defined, they may not always be obvious to all the players. Therefore, niche players may appear to compete. But, in practice, they do not do so or at least not fully (Rajagopal 2016). The area of operation or the size of the market also determines the consumer responsiveness and the effectiveness of delivery of goods and services. Thus, a follower in the large market may be the leader in the small market or niche. Smaller firms normally avoid competing with the larger firms. However, it has been observed that there is an increasing interest of big companies to serve the small area of operation or niche by setting up small business units. The niche strategy is profitable for the firms with low shares of the total market. The main reason is that the niche strategy provides total knowledge about the customer segment to the company to enable it to serve better through value addition. The niche marketing strategy provides *high margin* to the company, while the mass-marketing strategy may provide the advantage of *high volume* to the company. Companies operating in niche may consider the following strategies:

- Adequate size of the market
- Purchasing power of the segment to the tune of profitability
- Potential for growth
- Negligible interest to the competing companies
- Appropriate skills and resources to serve the niche in a superior fashion
- Well-knit defensive strategy to counter the competitors' attacks.

Most companies in their mature stage narrow down their portfolios and market segments to serve the customer effectively. In order to
remain successful in this stage, companies differentiate themselves from
other firms, either through price, product, marketing, distribution, or
service, in a narrower marketplace. Such strategy helps them build customer loyalty and stay competitive within niche (Linneman and Stanton
1991). In order to gain competitive advantage, firms tend to make their
niche market stronger and protected through product, brand, and services differentiation and clear geo-demographic segmentation. Mobile
phone companies operate in niche for a longer period and later open
their products and services to regional markets. Among many Chinese
mobile phone brands, Xiaomi, Huawei, Oppo, and One Plus are some
of the low-priced brands, which have grown their market in Asian niche
comprising India, Nepal, Sri Lanka, Thailand, Vietnam, and other
Southeast Asian countries. These brands have gradually opened their
niche and rolled-on to the Latin American market. In pursuing such
strategies, firms are practicing *open niche* strategies with the low price
high value dyadic effect, despite the fact that such strategies are identified
as disruptive marketing.

The most important issue in the niche marketing is specialization.
There are three major tasks to be attended by the companies looking
for developing the niche marketing strategy—creating a niche, expanding the niche, and protecting the niche markets. For example, Food and
Agriculture Organization (FAO) has identified the developing countries
as potential niche for the food and beverage markets. A study conducted
by FAO states that some 100 developing countries produce organic
commodities in commercial quantities, most of which are exported to
industrial countries (FAO 2003). It is also highlighted that developing
countries need assistance in complying with foreign standards and establishing international equivalency for a further expansion of supplies.
However, the niches are always risk-averse to the attacks of the competing
companies. The market niche also helps in encouraging the foreign direct
investment, with specific focus on the products and services (Rajagopal
2016). The formation of niche markets in the context of market entropy
is illustrated in Figure 2.1.

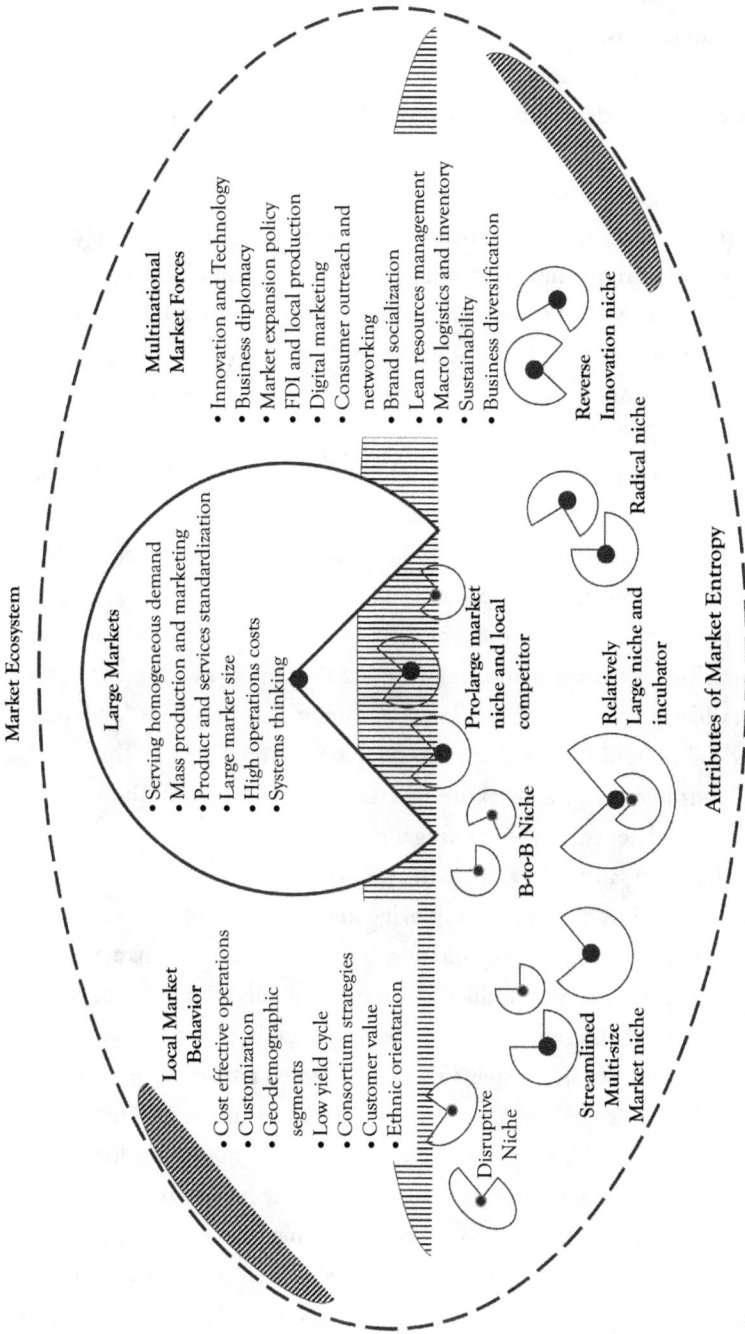

Figure 2.1 Market ecosystem and attributes of market entropy

Source: Author

Market ecosystem of multinational companies is changing rapidly in the dynamic consumption models across the industries today. Most companies create innovation- and technology-led demand within the proximity of their predetermined markets, which fragment overt time due to frugal innovations and local competitive strategies. Figure 2.1 illustrates that large markets in the context of the aforementioned business scenario tend to fragment into small niches and cannibalize the existing market share of large companies. Technology-driven companies like Apple Inc., Samsung, and Sony Inc. in the mobile phones industry have suffered setbacks in business performance over the years with the emergence of android communication operative system. Though Apple Inc. began its business operations in a niche market (geo-demographic), the boom of relatively low price-high value android phones of Samsung controlled the market expansion of iPhone in the decade of 2010. Over time, the market of mobile phones with an android operative system has been further segmented by low-price companies from China like Xiaomi, Huawei, and One Plus, which tended to cannibalize the market of Samsung mobile phones. This market scenario endorses that the sensitive customer touchpoints like innovation, technology, consumer surplus, price, and perceived values lead the large markets to fragment into niches. This value cycle continues until a breakthrough technology emerges. The market ecosystem is later controlled by frugal innovations.

Large companies develop their market initially to serve homogeneous demand and focus on achieving the economy of scale through mass-production and mass-marketing strategies. These companies tend to control costs though product and services standardization, operating in large market size, and adapting to the principle of systems thinking in *design-to-market* and systems selling processes. However, the existing market developed by large companies begins fragmenting into the product-specific or geo-demographic niches, as frugal innovations, low-price products, and customization practices grow in the local markets. Consequently, large companies realize incremental increase in the operations costs. Such business scenarios might trigger mergers and acquisitions of companies to manage further entropy in business and defection of consumers from the leading brands.

Figure 2.1 exhibits that niche market players adhere to cost-effective operations and carry out customization of their products and services to the possible extent within the geo-demographic segments. However, niche market players operate within a low-yield cycle and protect customer value. Various industries like consumer products and services, international technology, and business-to-business products are engaged in consortium manufacturing and marketing strategies to lower their cost of production and co-create products across destinations. The cooperative dairy industry in India and business-to-business products industries in China are good examples of consortium business strategies. Therefore, smaller firms, through consortium, pose challenge to larger firms by adapting multiple market disruption strategies like low prices, disruptive innovation, mass marketing, and building customer loyalty at the bottom of the pyramid segments (Rajagopal 2016). Companies continuously engaged in handling innovative business projects should periodically measure employee performance for the purpose of work force planning and also network broader collaborative contributions with other innovation management enterprises. Companies nurture innovation networks through talent management initiatives and systematic task allocation in carrying out innovative business project, for example, organizations including IDEO, IKEA, Dow Chemical, and Best Buy (Schweer et al. 2012).

As the large market fragments into niches, it boosts up local competition. These niche players are engaged in manufacturing and marketing lookalike products of large companies at relatively low prices with marginal differentiation in features and use values. Such niche companies lead to disruptive innovations and tend to cannibalize the market share of large companies through disruptive marketing strategies. Co-creating can also be considered as a disruptive strategy to some extent. Small companies with relatively older business, such as convenience stores or a group of companies in an industry, lead to streamlined market operations in extended market niches. Companies growing with diversified business operations in a niche also incubate new businesses in smaller niches. For example, Grupo Salinas in Mexico has incubated diversified business of manufacturing and retailing (Elektra), banking (Banco Azteca), Internet services (Total Play), and media channels (TV Azteca in alliance with Netflix Mexico). These incubated businesses have grown in respective niches in Mexico and across Latin American countries. Some niches grow independently in the marketplace engaged in frugal and reverse innovation activities. Radical niches sometimes emerge as social enterprises and co-create community products and services.

Small segments of consumers develop homogenous needs. Therefore, niche segments provide companies the opportunity to grow ethnic and socially distinctive brands. Such brands tend to have low market share and serve smaller customer base because of their specialized nature (Jarvis and Goodman 2005). Many buyers tend to have an alternative brand along with their preferred brand as a change of pace. The pace refers to the contextual attributes like time, vogue, and trends demonstrated in social buying behavior. This gives rise to potential large-share brands with derived loyalty, as a larger customer base reinforces its preferred choice. Therefore, a change-of-pace strategy captures only a limited share of the market, as consumers always look for an alternative brand to stay abreast with the vogue and social dynamics. Reinforcing brands in the niche market in such instances is relative to the competing brands (Kahn et al. 1988).

Retailing and Shopping Behavior

Consumers find the environment significantly positive, exhibit higher levels of approach and impulse buying behaviors, and experience enhanced satisfaction when the retail ambience is congruent with the arousing qualities (Mattila and Wirtz 2004). Visual effects associated with products often stimulate the buying decisions among young consumers. Point-of-sales brochures, catalogs, and posters build assumption on perceived use value and motivational relevance of buying decisions of product. Emotional visuals exhibited on contextual factors, such as proximity or stimulus size, drive perception and subjective reactions on utility and expected satisfaction of the products (Codispoti and De Cesarei 2007).

Personal shopping motives, values, and perceived shopping alternatives are often considered independent inputs to a choice model; it is argued that shopping motives influence the perception of retail store attributes as well as the attitude toward retail stores (Morschett et al. 2005). The recreational facilities prompt shopping arousal and play a pivotal role to deliver a divulging impact of buying behavior of young consumers. Shopping supported with recreational attractions may be identified as one of the major drivers in promoting tourism by demonstrating quality fashion products and store preferences to tourist shoppers. Arousal in shopping makes young consumers stay longer in the stores, experience the pleasure of products, and make buying decisions. Perceptions of shopping duration, emotional levels, and merchandise evaluations are derived from the level of arousal experienced by the consumers in the retail stores (Rajagopal 2007).

Retailers may address the various interests of the consumers through effective displays, designing appropriate retail ergonomics, easily identifiable packaging, making shopping exciting, and focusing in-store advertising to enhance arousal of young consumers (Quelch and Cannon-Bonventre 1983). The three distinct dimensions of emotions, which include pleasantness, arousal, and dominance, have been identified as major drivers for making buying decisions among adolescent consumers. The retail point of purchase is the time and place at which all the elements of a sale: the consumer, the money, and the product converge. Marketers must make the most of the communications possibilities at this point to increase their sales (Rajagopal 2006). There are some common strategies adopted by retailers to overcome the problems of fickle consumers, price-slashing competitors, and mood swings in the economy. Such perception holds that retailers can thrive only if they communicate better with young consumers through in-store amusement, recreation, and collaborative product demonstrations involving consumers, to help in their purchase decisions. Retailers also offer buying incentives to develop conviction on buying such tried out products (Berry 2001).

The retailing industry in emerging markets is growing fast and has reached the edge of competition by making shopping malls attractive to consumers and inducing their consumption culture. Word-of-mouth and digital marketing have emerged as strong drivers for motivating consumers to visit shopping malls and inculcate value. Marketplaces in urban demographic settings attract a large number of buyers and sellers, which can be termed as market thickness. Co-existence of many shopping malls along with traditional markets in a marketplace causes market *mobbing* (Wadud and Chen 2018). Retailing companies compete within the industry to achieve market leadership by creating hedonic values to consumers while shopping in supermarkets and shopping malls. The utilitarian values of consumers in buying affect their decision, but recreational amenities in retail outlets meaningfully supplement the latent hedonic motives of consumers. The recreational services, therefore, augment consumer perceptions and values toward intensive shopping in retail outlets (Ryu et al. 2010).

Market competition in the retailing industry is growing rapidly in emerging markets. However, social and economic differences exist within hedonic shopping behaviors in both developed and developing countries. Advertising and the atmosphere within retail stores have also gained importance over the years, as digital marketing technology has improved and become cost-effective. In the Internet era, retailing attributes like creating purchase incentives, in-store ergonomics and consumer orientation, and store location play a significant role in attracting consumers. The retailing model in a market for differentiated goods varies in reference to destinations, shopping malls, and retailing platforms. The ambience of shopping malls and retail outlets depends on the size of the marketplace. Large marketplaces offer competitive prices, which are often low and linked with creative promotions. Such attributes of retailing in large shopping malls not only increase the inflow of consumers, but also lead to higher profits among the retailing firms (Parakhonyak and Titova 2018; Blut et al. 2018).

Retailing is widely associated with the variety-seeking behavior of consumers. Shopping malls that have extensive assortment of shops and pleasant and attractive ambience attract customers. However, convenience of the shopping mall and the communication activities also act as pull factors. Thus, consumer convenience, tenant variety, product specialization, internal environment, and leisure and communication play a major role in elevating the brand of a shopping mall or store as a retailing icon among the consumers (Calvo-Porral and Lévy-Mangín 2018). A larger shopping center accommodates a wider assortment of shops and creates a leisure shopping environment for the consumers, which allures shoppers to stay longer in the mall. Both the utilitarian and hedonic shopping values affect a customer's lifestyle while shopping in a mall. Sustainable shopping values are delivered by the shopping malls through administering consumer-centric strategies efficiently. The values generated through co-creation help in developing satisfaction among the shoppers. Retailers can design the mall ambience ergonomically by understanding and analyzing the shopping values of consumers (Kesari and Atulkar 2016).

Suburbanization has been driven by the development of large suburban shopping malls and retail parks. The image of shopping malls transforms the image of the stores located in the mall, as shoppers develop self-congruity and anthropomorphic behavior in shopping at these malls. In addition, the image dimensions of a shopping mall influence the hedonic shopping value through self-image congruity. The dimensions of stores image within the shopping mall influence the utilitarian and hedonic shopping values. Both types of shopping values are strong drivers of mall patronage (Hedhli et al. 2017). Large retail chains in an urban and suburban habitat and assorted retail stores in the malls entice consumers through value-added recreational services and enhance shopping experiences. However, small retailers can harness consumer relationship through social interaction. Fast-moving consumer goods manufacturing and marketing companies use the competitive strength of small retailers to understand market demand and increase their distribution in the interiors of the country. It is observed that large and recreational shopping malls attract regular shoppers and tourists toward frequent shopping. Accordingly, most of the growing cities are patronizing their suburban shopping malls and power centers, rather than downtown market places (Khare 2014).

With the advancement of innovative retailing strategies, transformative retail service (TRS) is emerging as sustainable business practice in the industry. TRS is designed to increase the satisfaction and loyalty of customers by inculcating the emotions of well-being in shopping. The impact of transformative retail services on customer well-being elevates loyalty, purchase intentions, and brand-related appeals through unique sales propositions of retail promotions (Troebs et al. 2018). The theory of shopping provides insights on the consumer behavioral perspectives in reference to need, desire, and satisfaction. However, shopping as a behavioral phenomenon varies in the context of everyday basic activities.

Shopping is primarily concerned with individuals and materialism. This assumption has been re-examined and reviewed in previous studies, which argues shopping behavior from the anthropological perspective and hedonic values. The act of purchasing goods is often linked to social relations, especially those based on love and care (Miller 2013). Shopping in the contemporary context is viewed as a blend of hedonistic and utilitarian consumption philosophies. Hedonism is the prioritizing of pleasure over other life values and is theorized to be independent of well-being, which a consumer would like to perceive during the course of shopping. The value-based hedonist shoppers have a distinct moral profile, as they are less likely to endorse moral foundations associated with social conservatism. However, shoppers with an excessive pleasure-seeking behavior form a premier segment in the society.

Consumers who value pleasure have a distinct, socially liberal moral profile, and the tendency to pursue hedonic pleasure is reflected in their personality. Hedonism can be viewed in two distinctive perspectives that affect the behavior of consumers toward shopping. People who have ultimate desires regarding their own hedonic states referring to pleasure and pain hold the inferential hedonism. On the other hand, reinforcement of hedonism focuses on the ultimate desires of consumers, irrespective of differential values in that person's cognitive system only by virtue of their association with predetermined hedonic states. This theory endorses that consumers tend to visit shopping malls with ultra-modern facilities and categorically positioned in the society with premium values (Garson 2016).

Another school of thought argues pro-value perspectives of consumer behavior support the utilitarian philosophy of consumption. Accordingly, the value-based theory of shopping argues that consumers favor utilitarian features over hedonic features in an explicit acquisition choice. Previous research studies have shown that, although the hedonic shopping feature is more valued by users, it is the utilitarian behavior of shoppers that governs in the mass-consumption situations. The behavior of consumers toward shopping malls is driven by several utilitarian motivations concerning assortment of stores, buying economy, convenience, availability of information, customization, desire for modernity, payment services, anonymity and security, and selective social interaction (Kakar 2017).

Consumers prefer to shop in the malls that also serve as utilitarian buying centers besides offering the recreational and hedonic values.

Simulated Chaos

The market ecosystem today is not stable, as it is driven by the high inflow of frugal innovations, dynamic pricing strategies, and changing consumer behavior. The digital consumer networks have increased communication outreach across the geo-demographic segments. A small change in the marketing strategy in one product portfolio to specific target consumers affects the preferences of consumers in larger geo-demographic segments across destinations. Such market effect can be described as simulated chaos in small markets. Innovations in the niche markets play a major role in stimulating the demand in the global markets, which is caused by effective commercialization of reverse innovations. The faster delivery of medical supplies in remote areas through Zipline drones in African Skies (Rwanda and Ghana) and portable electrocardiogram (ECG) machines that help doctors diagnose in clinics in rural India are the milestones of reverse innovations that carried out the butterfly effect in the global markets. These niche experiments have been reviewed by the global companies and commercialized the innovations, for example, drone medical supply deliveries (Zipline in Bostia and Ghana) and portable ECG machine (General Electric Company with brand name GE Mac 400). Likewise, an off-road wheelchair called Leveraged Freedom Chair (LFC), which is 80 percent faster and 40 percent more efficient to propel than a conventional wheelchair in India, sells for approximately 250 U.S. dollars on par with the products of other developing countries. The technologies that generate its high performance and low cost have been incorporated into a western version, manufactured by the Global Research Innovation and Technology, Inc. This product is branded as the GRIT Freedom Chair, which was modified with consumer feedback and sells in the United States for 3,295 U.S. dollars, less than half the price of competing products. Many competitors are emerging across the emerging markets in the product segment (Winter and Govindarajan 2015). These examples explain the niche effects of innovation in larger markets emerge as the butterfly effect over time.

Digital health is an emerging platform for reverse innovation, as it encourages inexpensive, easy-to-use, and innovative products that are affordable to consumers. Consumer care is usually developed as high-technology high-price products by the companies that do not often stand competitive in the market. Frugal innovations with the perspectives of applied consumer values attract the mass market. However, the cost-effective and price-competitive products soon tend to cause chaos in the market due to emergence of oligopolistic markets. Reverse innovations emerging in the service sector also drive the butterfly effect and tend to simulate the chaotic situations in a niche market. The success of Mashavu Project in delivering telemedicine to Kenya and Tanzania has driven a global attraction for new companies to adapt to Mashavu social enterprise model. Tapping the creativity and social activism of college students and keeping equipment costs down are being experimented in various niches in developing countries in Southeast Asia.

Butterfly effects are sensitive to the market environment to grow and make impact. Companies that are enjoying the monopoly or near-monopoly market conditions hold better opportunities to trigger small changes to gain profits in the market at a larger scale. However, in oligopolistic market conditions, small changes in products, services, processes, and strategies largely drive tactical gains to a company and call for short consumer responses. In order to make the butterfly effect sustainable, companies need to introduce changes in phases in the market backed by effective communication to stimulate consumers to accept the changes in products and services.

Large companies believe in dynamic marketing and tend to improve their product portfolios through continuous innovations. Every innovation—total, partial, or cosmetic—to a product attracts competitors. Over time, all innovative improvements are susceptible to chaos in a niche market. This situation may also spread over the neighboring markets if the demand is stimulated simultaneously in these markets and deliver higher advantages to the consumers in contemporary market competition. Competitive firms intend to engage in a continuous organizational learning process with respect to the value creation chain and measure performance of the new products introduced in the market (Rajagopal 2015). In the growing competitive markets, large and reputed firms are developing differentiation strategies to move into the mass markets by combining innovation and changes in the products and services as *high-value integrated solutions* tailored to each customer's needs than simply *moving downstream* into services. Such firms are developing innovative combinations of service capabilities such as operations, business consultancy, and finance required to drive the butterfly effect in business by providing complete solutions to each customer's needs in order to augment customer value toward the innovative or new products. It has been argued that the provision of integrated solutions is to attract firms traditionally based in manufacturing and services to occupy a new base in the value stream centered on *systems integration* using internal or external sources of product designing, supply, and customer-focused promotion (Davies 2004). Besides the organizational perspectives of enhancing the customer value for any change introduced by the company, the functional variables like pricing play a significant role in developing the customer perceptions toward the new products. The two core concepts of the competitor learning process are *efficient and effective* learning. The former refers to the learning input–output ratio. The input for the learning process is the competitor data, and the output includes the change in the knowledge level. The effective competitor learning addresses the output–decision relationship. In the process of competitor learning, both efficiency and effectiveness need attention and require data, information, and intelligence. Marketplace rules can be changed at three distinct but related levels: the aggregate marketplace or, more narrowly, a competitive domain; a product-customer segment such as a niche within a competitive domain; and local channel member. All rivalry is ultimately acted out at the local or micro level. Each individual customer selects among rivals' offerings. At this level, the game is typically zero-sum: purchasing one rival's offering means lost opportunity for the other competitors. Firms generally make the choices that have been experienced in the past by the competitors to accomplish three distinct, though related, tasks, including attracting, winning, and retaining customers and channels. Attracting customers is a prelude to winning or acquiring them. The brand name and long-standing image of the product influence and attracts customers to try a product (Rajagopal 2019).

Learning market dynamics and improving organizational capabilities add value to innovative thinking and develop different competitive mind-set and a systematic way of looking for opportunities. Companies should look ahead of the conventional boundaries so that managers can look methodically across the strategies employed by the competitors in the marketplace. By doing so, companies can find new market space to establish their brand and business and position real-value innovation. Some companies also engage in introspecting their capabilities and competencies rather than looking at competitors by encouraging managers to ask themselves why customers make the trade-off between substitute products or services. Home Depot, a U.S. house constructions and utilities chain store, for example, analyzed the existing market competition serving home improvement and developed products and services differentiations to enhance the customer value. Upon critically appraising its own strategies, the company derived powerful insights by reviewing familiar data from a new perspective. Similar insights can be analyzed by looking across strategic groups within an industry, across buyer groups, across complementary product and service offerings, across the functional-emotional orientation of an industry, and even across time (Kim and Mauborgne 1999).

Knowledge management involves many procedures and techniques used to get the most from an organization's explicit and tacit know-how. Information acquisition, sharing of knowledge among the employees in the organization, and diffusing experience and analytical skills within the organization form the core activities of knowledge management. Sharing knowledge without personal bias among peers or employees within the organization is the most important critical success factor of all knowledge management strategies. Effective knowledge sharing practices allow individuals to reuse and regenerate knowledge at the individual and organizational level (Chaudhry 2005). However, most enterprises observe individual and organizational barriers in knowledge sharing that include internal resistance, trust, motivation, and inadequate awareness. Learning organizations require a change in focus from a technology-driven approach to a people-driven approach in order to improve knowledge management. With the evolution of technology, the paradigm of knowledge management is shifting from a conventional approach to an analytical approach as a conversational medium by combining formal and informal knowledge within a social context (Hong 2011). Learning organizations can effectively acquire knowledge and skills through formal and on-market learning opportunities and develop need-based product innovation and improvement skills. However, most organizations fail to build logical frameworks for learning and push their employees to engage in a trial-and-error process for gaining the right market-oriented innovation vision. However, the most effective ways of continuous learning occur in organizations through shared vision, systems thinking, and team learning.

Transforming markets for adapting product and services innovations is a big challenge for most companies engaged in doing business in consumer products. Innovative products need to be transformed to the perceived suitability of consumers for optimal use by way of total customization. Most innovative products have the limitation for 360-degree transformation due to the standardized functionality and built-in structural restrictions. Companies willing to drive change in the marketplace in the context of demand and consumer behavior have traditionally come through top-down initiatives such as corporate endorsements toward manufacturing design, quality, and technology. Critical innovations in consumer products like light emitting diode (LED) screens and lighting devices have transformed consumer behavior and market demand to get more value at less price. Transforming buying behavior for such innovations is relatively easier than educating consumers toward the use of innovation in educational products and services. But, within every organization, there are a few product innovations that encounter unique marketing problems that seem impossible to solve. Although these change agent products in a company roll out in the market with effective communication tools to drive awareness, attractiveness, trial, availability, and repeat buying stimulus, they often fail to gain consumer confidence in usability and so fail to generate the desired response in the market.

Companies can develop innovation launch and transformation strategies to stimulate consumer preferences. To work with such strategies, companies need to consider the following attributes:

- Co-create community orientation and engage the process of self-appraisal of innovative products and services in terms of competitive benefits and value for money

- Reframe innovation through facts and prepare for innovation transformation according to customer needs and market demand
- Entail marketing of innovative products in the existing channel network and allow direct marketing to create customer value
- Make innovation safe to learn among consumers and market players by creating an environment that builds constructive opinions
- Grow communication grapevine through the digital networks and physical community infrastructure on the innovations and competitive advantages
- Make the innovations as problem solver and drive them in the market as a key to the community satisfaction
- Leverage social evidences for the innovation considering its applications to the larger community-led consumer awareness like ecofriendly detergents that minimize cesspool and soil pollution
- Build immunity to innovations in the market against disruptions and misevaluations that could build low trust and commitment among the consumers and market players

Companies should ensure that throughout these steps, they must adopt a facilitator's role without overpowering the consumers or raising conflicts with the competitors. Such corporate attitude may cause damage to the brand image of the company. The customer-centric innovation transformation methodology can help in solving even the most extreme dilemmas on innovation acceptability in the market and its socialization for sustained growth (Pascale and Sternin 2005). Cultivating continual innovation and creating new business models have become the essential success parameters of any business. Vertical and horizontal integrations are imperative to the success of a corporation, resulting in the models that provide tremendous business opportunities. This approach also brings great execution challenges. In addition to creating innovation through internal research and development, two significant areas where enterprises constantly strive to create innovative capabilities are mergers and acquisitions and partner strategies. Innovation and new business models can be successfully enabled through connecting specific products and solutions. A robust network foundation is essential for building higher-level infrastructure services. This foundation includes intelligent network capabilities at the different network locations, including branch offices, campus, external connectivity, and home and partner environments. A converged network infrastructure can result in major savings when collaboration and video are enabled along with the right productivity solutions, *for example,* using unified communications and collaboration technologies, immersive video and video phones. A key technical requirement to scale business models is the faster service provisioning. Through the use of a private cloud and intelligent automation solutions, corporations can reduce the time taken to provision a new service. Embracing virtual desktop technologies can also result in considerable advantages.

Broadly, innovation is considered as an intellectual accomplishment at the grassroots of humanity, but commercializing it is a business skill compounded with capabilities, competencies, and resources of the organizations. Thus, most business innovations are either developed by micro, small, or medium enterprises, but they lead to mergers or acquisition with a larger business organization to gain enough resources to grow in a marketplace. Most of the innovations driving potential businesses are acquired by the large companies and carried forward to develop them commercially and position them sustainably in the marketplace. For example, in small information technology companies, young software developers have worked on developing the interactive shopper software to support the consumers on selecting clothing and dresses that are suitable to their appearance and taste online. This software has been later made available for personal computers, local area networks, android phones, and many more devices. The virtual dressing room can be installed in any place that has electricity and broadband Internet access, and the developers hope to eventually see the unit installed in areas like train stations and airport terminals.

Most product differentiations exhibit some form of risk in competition. There are some firms that can drive consumer attention in competitive markets and create competitive advantage. Operating on economies of scale for a large firm may also have a significant competitive advantage to drive changes, as it may enjoy a large volume of production at lower costs, which may further lead to the price leadership with low retail prices. Such strategy would also prevent the potential competitors from entering the business. An incumbent firm may make it hard for a would-be entrant by incurring huge sunk costs with high-budget advertising. In view of such strategy, any new differentiation may match to compete effectively in the market, but have low market share during the initial period. However, this situation is alarming for the companies as the sunk costs incurred on advertising or researching a product idea may be huge and irrecoverable. Another radical strategy used by the powerful firms to discourage consumer-switching behavior is by raising exit costs such as product insurance, warranty and guarantee terms, and product exchange policies. Thus, firms can earn some excess profits by making the differentiated products to compete with those of rival companies by bringing down the prices.

Demand Fragmentation, Consumer Defection, and Price Entropy

Consumer demand for products and services is widely stimulated by the functional factors in marketing that include price, availability, efficiency in delivery of products, promotions strategies, and customer services. In a competitive marketplace, companies within the industry develop marketing strategies to attract consumers using the strategies on the earlier-referred consumer touchpoints. Consequently, the demand for the similar (marginally differentiated products) and identical products creates chaos in the market, causing defection of consumers across the brands. Local enterprises can reduce the prices to gain quick increase in market share for the remanufactured products, focusing marketing and sales strategies on the sustainability concerns. Lowering the prices drives the consumer purchase intentions and sets major challenges toward the price competition in the local and global markets. Low-price products create a chaotic environment in the marketplace due to inconsistency of referrals, consumer value perceptions, and switching cost leverage across the brands. Retailers sell remanufactured and new products, as all market players are concerned about improving the supply chain performance for sustainability. Sustainability is a relatively new concept that defines the pricing strategy as a function of triple bottom line pertaining to economy, environment, and social values (Bottani et al. 2015). Therefore, pricing has emerged as a vital competitive tool for distributors and manufacturers to attract customers. In addition to low price, companies encourage customers to exhibit their interest toward the price–quality relationship to make their brands more competitive against the high-price products. Consequently, the brands of large companies targeting mass markets tend to raise their price competitiveness by keeping the price at par with, or lower than, the competitors. The attributes of demand fragmentation, consumer defection, and price entropy are exhibited in Figure 2.2.

Functional disorientation in marketing is caused due to the fragmentation of demand for a product or service over time with the growing competition in the marketplace, as illustrated in Figure 2.2. Commonly, demand fragmentation is experienced in the fashion products, frugal innovation, mass-market consumer products and services in their growth stage due to increase in competition and unwarranted shifts in the consumer behavior. Large companies create demand or their products at the macro-market level by employing resources on various marketing-mix elements spread across 11Ps that include product, price, place promotion, packaging, pace, performance, people, psychodynamics, posture, and proliferation. Implementing a long-term strategy on these marketing-mix elements enhances the scope of latitudinal expansion of markets. Most companies employ push strategies with a focus on competitive pricing and promotions, aggressive advertisements, social media referrals, and services to enhance market demand. Companies drive mass consumers toward high-end brands of the premium segments by sensitizing consumer touchpoints embedding strategies on the price, promotion, packaging, performance, psychodynamics, and corporate reputation (posture). Such efforts of companies help in increasing the sales and market share of their products and services; however, aggressive push strategies trigger chaotic market competition of similar products and services, causing high substitution effect on the other. The price-linked demand sensitivity drives substitutability of products, which leads to demand fragmentation. Over time, local brands further segregate the demand, attract customers by offering higher value for money, and deliver consumer surplus. In

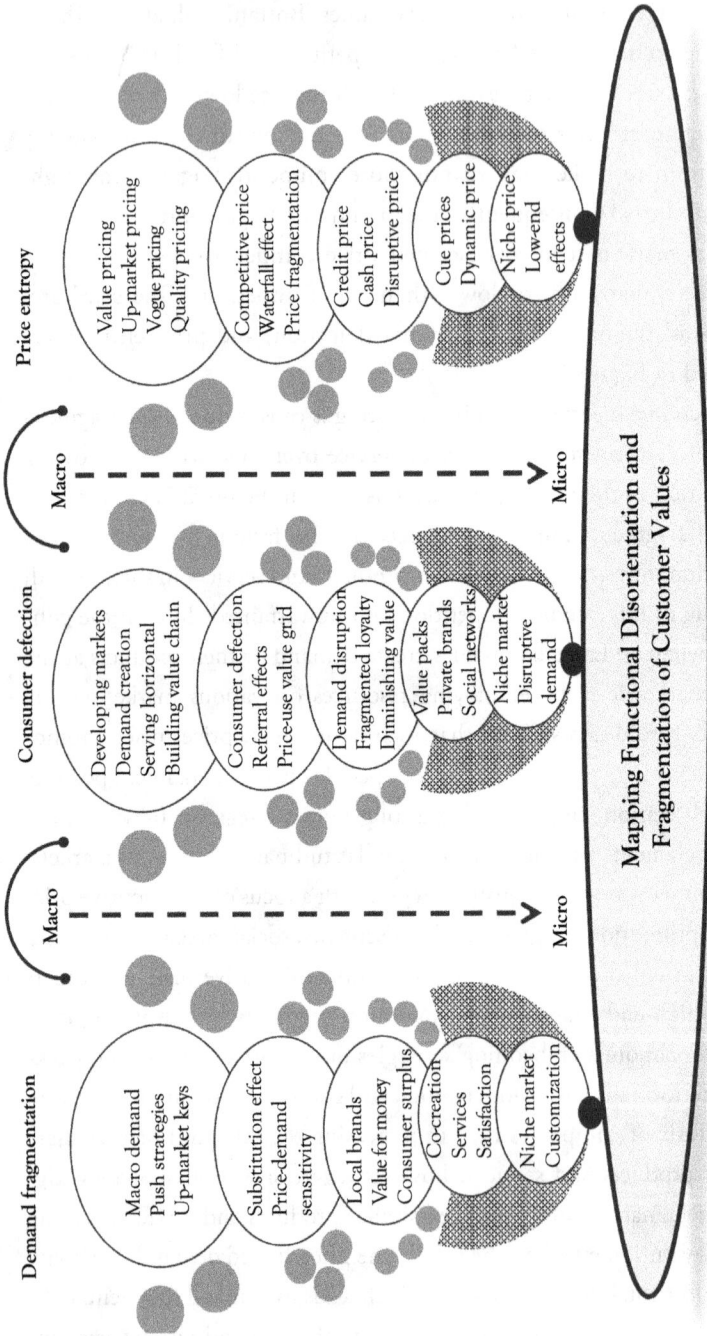

Figure 2.2 Functional factors entropy in marketing

Source: Author

addition, co-creation and customization of products and services stimulate the demand at the bottom of the pyramid in the niche markets.

Customer defection is a discrete process across brands in the competitive marketplace. Large consumer products companies often employ long-term strategies in developing consumerism for their brands by creating demand and serving the demand across geo-demographic segments. These companies invest in building a value chain through personalized customer services. However, the negative consumer referrals and price-value dissatisfactions lead to consumer defections, as illustrated in Figure 2.2. In addition, the diminishing perceived values among consumers cause fragmentation in the loyalty due to disruption of demand. Low-price brands often create such disruption. The value packs of products and services offered by the private brands, and peer interactions on social networks encourage brand defections. Accordingly, the customer loyalty to large markets is gradually fragmented and confined to niche markets.

Price fragmentation across consumer segments and markets also affect the demand disruption and customer defection. As companies drive mass-market sales attracting mass and bottom-of-the-pyramid segment, prices are offered with higher value for money. The quality-linked pricing in up-markets also tends to fragment across the destination markets. Most companies set incremental markup based on the price waterfall paradigm, which provides higher profit on higher price for the products in early period of their launch, and companies compromise lower profits at declining prices over time as the demand gradually tends to decline. In the competitive marketplace, consumers experience attractive products frequently, exhibit varied preferences, lean toward dynamic motivations, and show inconsistency in propensity to spend. Most competitors set competitive prices and develop short-term pricing strategies to gain quick profit in the market. However, successful companies follow a pricing pattern by understanding the purchasing power of the consumers, uniqueness of the products, and the brand value associated with the products. Such pricing strategy is identified as a price waterfall paradigm, which guides the companies to set appropriate price in reference to the demand and purchasing power of the consumers. In this pricing model, the highest possible price is set for the products during the initial launch in the premium or mass-consumer segment. Companies also invest in product demonstration and advertising during this period, to attract consumers. Companies continuously track the sales performance of the products during this stage of pricing, and a discounted price is set to attract consumers as the demand begins to decline. The demand trend and the volume of sales are continuously monitored, and different price levels are set until the product fetches maximum sales. The price at such point of sales is known as harvest price, which is set as the base price for the new season sales (Rajagopal 2019).

Figure 2.2 also shows that the growing cash discounts on products and services, the increasing credit transactions on buying, and the escalating disruptive prices of imitated brands also cause serious implications in the markets. These attributes not only lead the demand and price disruptions, but also stay responsible to consumer defection across the brands. Cue pricing strategy, which stays the same for long time, also disrupts the markets and drives defection across the completing brands. For example, Nirma, a low-end market, multi-purpose detergent brand in India, with its cue pricing strategy that maintained the price of INR 10 (approximately 0.26 U.S. dollars at the then prices) for a kilogram over a decade. This brand had caused consumer defection across the brands of multinational companies in the Indian marketplace between mid-1980s and 1990s.

Empirical studies have shown that the mass markets have higher number of consumers than those cater to the premium consumers segment. The former type of markets consistently deliver higher market share and risk-adjusted returns, and the latter type of markets operate on a predetermined price-profit matrix. Therefore, fragmentation of demand and price is more frequent in mass markets than the markets that serve premium segments. However, companies serving the premium consumer segment that attempt to envelop the mass markets for enhancing their market share cause fragmentation of price and demand. Such market expansion strategy leads to brand defections within the product portfolios of a company and drives cannibalization within the product line. For example, automobile companies introducing various brands with marginal differentiation in price and internal ergonomics, often segregate consumer preferences toward a specific model affecting the market share of other models within the product portfolio. In addition, customer defection also spreads across the competing brands of similar attributes and use value. Companies develop these skills through learning and potentially experiencing marketing of unprofitable brands along the product portfolios (Ladley et al. 2015). Market decentralization since the beginning of the 21st century has guided the companies to increase the product line in profitable product portfolios. In response to such strategy, market competition has simultaneously grown, disrupting the existing demand and causing consumer defection.

The growing acquaintance of consumers with innovation and technology shows that consumers are able to co-create and self-produce both meaningful contents and tangible outputs. These activities do not affect most of the traditional marketplaces, and in fact, consumers may even express a co-destructive rather than co-creative tendency. However, consumers in some product segments, such as digital products, foster the emergence of new creative practices and innovations (Arnould 2014). Recent research studies on market system dynamics highlight that consumers not only possess the capacity to affect the market demand, but also play a role in envisioning and creating new markets. Therefore, in addition to the role of modifiers of an existing market, consumers also play the role of consumer-entrepreneurs, affecting marketplaces that might cause defection of consumers over the low-yielding brands (Giesler and Fischer 2016). Markets today not only provide multiple goods and services to the customers, but also stimulate their behavior to the cross-cultural products, services, and innovations. The specialization of the production process has also brought such cultural changes by business penetrations in the low-production skills regions across countries. Apparel from Asian countries like Indonesia and Korea, all types of consumer goods from China, electronics from Japan, and perfumery from France may be some good examples to explain the specialization and cross-cultural sharing of consumer behavior. Conducting business is a creative enterprise, and doing it out of one's own country is more demanding (Rajagopal 2019).

Summary

Market entropy broadly refers to the fragmentation of markets from larger markets to niche markets. The advancement of innovation and technology along the growth in market competition has driven the conventional markets to fragment in small niches across specialized products and services and geo-demographic segments. Companies with their specialized product portfolios have delivered higher values to customers and created loyalty than competing on a less-known marketplace with more competitors. Such marketing philosophy has driven most companies to choose an appropriate niche to develop consistency in market share, profitability, and business growth. However, over time, the radical changes in consumer preferences have led to shifts in consumption patterns, causing fragmentation in the conventional markets. Accordingly, the retailing and shopping behaviors of consumers have also showed inconsistency toward brand loyalty, buying attitude, and referrals. Such market situation has caused instability in the market ecosystem and turned it susceptible to unwarranted changes. The contemporary market ecosystem is driven by the high inflow of frugal innovations, dynamic pricing strategies, and frequent changes in the consumer behavior. The informal market information among the consumers drive brand defections and demand fragmentation across marketplaces. A small change in consumer behavior or corporate strategy might cause a large latitudinal impact, which may be described as the butterfly effect. Frequent occurrences of such effects lead to simulated chaos in the marketplace causing market entropy.

Hybrid business cultures are emerging across industries. The regional businesses are emerging with consumers as partners and growing global, for example, IKEA, a Swedish company, which has grown its brand globally as a *co-creation* business house. Evolution of niche market companies across geo-demographic segments (domestic delivery services and digital dinning and leisure platforms) is a phenomenon that often reflects deep structural changes in the progressive business models. It usually takes a long time to unfold benefits of hybrid businesses, as comparative advantages in such fragmented business models appear in long term. The structural reforms in emerging markets have broadly focused in five major areas comprising consumer products marketing, financial markets, digital markets, and the generation and use of community platforms. Consequently, market development appears to be a wider challenge, and companies need to understand the attribute and depth of probable entropy.

References

Arnould, E.J. 2014. "Rudiments of a Value Praxeology." *Marketing Theory* 14, no. 1, pp. 129–33.

Berry, L.L. 2001. "The Old Pillars of New Retailing." *Harvard Business Review* 79, no. 4, pp. 131–37.

Blut, M., C. Teller, and A. Floh. 2018. "Testing Retail Marketing-Mix Effects on Patronage: A Meta-Analysis." *Journal of Retailing* 94, pp. 113–35.

Bottani, E., R. Montanari, M. Rinaldi, and G. Vignali. 2015. "Modeling and Multi-Objective Optimization of Closed Loop Supply Chains: A Case Study." *Computers & Industrial Engineering* 87, pp. 328–42.

Calvo-Porral, C., and J.P. Lévy-Mangín. 2018. "Pull Factors of the Shopping Malls: An Empirical Study." *International Journal of Retail and Distribution Management* 46, pp. 110–24.

Chaudhry, A.S. 2005. "Knowledge Sharing Practices in Asian Institutions: A Multi-Cultural Perspective from Singapore." In *Proceedings of 71th IFLA General Conference and Council*. Oslo, Norway.

Codispoti, M., and A. De Cesarei. 2007. "Arousal and Attention: Picture Size and Emotional Reactions." *Psychophysiology* 44, pp. 680–86.

Dalgic, T., and M. Leeuw. 1994. "Niche Marketing Revisited: Concept, Applications and Some European Cases." *European Journal of Marketing* 28, pp. 39–55.

Davies, A. 2004. "Moving Base into High-Value Integrated Solutions: A Value Stream Approach." *Industrial and Corporate Change* 13, pp. 727–56.

FAO. 2003. *The State of Food and Agriculture*. Rome: Food and Agricultural Organization.

Garson, J. 2016. "Two Types of Psychological Hedonism." *Studies in History and Philosophy of Biological and Biomedical Sciences* 56, pp. 7–14.

Giesler, M., and E. Fischer. 2016. "Market System Dynamics." *Marketing Theory* 17, pp. 3–8.

Hammervoll, T., P. Mora, and K. Toften. 2013. "The Financial Crisis and the Wine Industry: The Performance of Niche Firms versus Mass-Market Firms." *Wine Economics and Policy* 3, pp. 108–14.

Hammervoll, T. 2014. "Service Provision for Co-creation of Value: Insights from Exchange- and Production Economy Perspectives." *International Journal of Physical Distribution & Logistics Management* 44, nos. 1–2, pp. 155–168.

Hong, D., E. Suh, and C. Koo. 2011. "Developing Strategies for Overcoming Barriers to Knowledge Sharing Based on Conversational Knowledge Management: A Case Study of a Financial Company." *Expert Systems with Applications* 38, pp. 14417–27.

Jarvis, W., and S. Goodman. 2005. "Effective Marketing of Small Brands: Niche

Positions, Attribute Loyalty and Direct Marketing."*Journal of Product & Brand Management* 14, pp. 292–99.

Kahn, B., M. Kalwani, and D. Morrison. 1988. "Niching versus Change of Pace Brands: Using Purchase Frequencies and Penetration Rates to Infer Brand Positioning." *Journal of Marketing Research* 25, pp. 384–90.

Kakar, A.K.S. 2017. "Why Do Users Prefer the Hedonic but Choose the Utilitarian? Investigating User Dilemma of Hedonic-Utilitarian Choice." *International Journal of Human-Computer Studies* 108, pp. 50–61.

Kesari, B., and S. Atulkar. 2016. "Satisfaction of Mall Shoppers: A Study on Perceived Utilitarian and Hedonic Shopping Values." *Journal of Retailing and Consumer Services* 31, pp. 22–31.

Khare, A. 2014. "Consumer-Small Retailer Relationships in Indian Retail." *Facilities* 32, pp. 533–53.

Kim, W.C., and R. Mauborgne. 1999. "Creating New Market Space. *Harvard Business Review* 77, pp. 83–93.

Ladley, D., T. Lensberg, J. Palczewski, and K.R. Schenk-Hoppé. 2015. "Fragmentation and Stability of Markets." *Journal of Economic Behavior & Organization* 119, pp. 466–81.

Linneman, R.E., and J.L. Stanton. 1991. *Making Niche Marketing Work: How to Grow Bigger by Acting Smaller*. New York, NY: McGraw Hill, Inc.

Mattila, A.S., and J. Wirtz. 2004. "Congruency of Scent and Music as a Driver of In-Store Evaluations and Behavior." *Journal of Retailing* 77, pp. 273–89.

Miller, D. (2013). *The Dialectics of Shopping*. Lewis Henry Morgan Lecture Series, Chicago: IL, University of Chicago Press.

Morschett, D., B. Swoboda, and T. Foscht. 2005. "Perception of Store Attributes and Overall Attitude towards Grocery Retailers: The Role of Shopping Motives." *The International Review of Retail, Distribution and Consumer Research* 15, pp. 423–47.

Parakhonyak, A., and M. Titova. 2018. "Shopping Malls, Platforms and Consumer Search." *International Journal of Industrial Organization* 58, pp. 183–213.

Pascale, R.T., and J Sternin. 2005. "Your Company´s Secret Change Agents." *Harvard Business Review* 83, pp. 72–81.

Quelch, J.A., and K. Cannon-Bonventre. 1983. "Better Marketing at the Point of Purchase." *Harvard Business Review* 61, pp. 162–69.

Rajagopal. 2006. "Leisure Shopping Behavior and Recreational Retailing: A Symbiotic Analysis of Marketplace Strategy and Consumer Response." *Journal of Hospitality and Leisure Marketing* 15, pp. 5–31.

Rajagopal. 2007. "Stimulating Retail Sales and Upholding Customer Value." *Journal of Retail and Leisure Property* 6, pp. 117–35.

Rajagopal. 2010. "Coexistence and Conflicts between Shopping Malls and Street Markets in Growing Cities: Analysis of Shoppers™ Behavior." *Journal of Retail and Leisure Property* 9, pp. 277–301.

Rajagopal. 2019. *Contemporary Marketing Strategy: Analyzing Consumer Behavior to Drive Managerial Decision Making.* New York: Palgrave Macmillan.

Ryu, K., H. Han, and S.S. Jang. 2010. "Relationships among Hedonic and Utilitarian Values Satisfaction and Behavioral Intentions in the Fast-Casual Restaurant Industry." *International Journal of Contemporary Hospitality Management* 22, pp. 416–32.

Schweer, M., D. Assimakopoulos, R. Cross, and R.J Thomas. 2012. "Building a Well-Networked Organization." *MIT Sloan Management Review* 53, no. 2.

Toften, K., and T Hammervoll. 2013. "Niche Marketing Research: Status and Challenges." *Marketing Intelligence & Planning* 31, pp. 272–85.

Troebs, C.C., T. Wagner, and F Heidemann. 2018. "Transformative Retail Services: Elevating Loyalty through Customer Well-Being." *Journal of Retailing and Consumer Services* 45, pp. 198–206.

Wadud, Z., and D Chen. 2018. "Congestion Impacts of Shopping Using Vehicle Tracking Data." *Journal of Transport Geography* 70, pp. 123–30.

Winter, A., and V Govindarajan. 2015. "Engineering Reverse Innovation." *Harvard Business Review* 93, pp. 80–89.

CHAPTER 3

Innovation and Technology

Overview

Growth of innovation and technology-led products is faster than their adaptation among the consumers. Innovations at the bottom-of-the-pyramid market segments possess attributes of low cost, price competitive, and high value for money. This chapter discusses the causes of innovation boom in consumer-centric and industrial products and its effects on market entropy. High competition and industry rivalry of low-cost innovations in consumer and business-to-business market segments cause chaos, demand fragmentation, consumer defection, and drift to niche markets. Attributes of incremental innovation and reverse innovation and their changing market potential have been discussed in this chapter. Discussions are also central to the breakthrough innovations in the context of their market potential and effects on large markets. The lifecycle of innovation in the context of market chaos and demand fragmentation has been discussed in the chapter to explain the concept of market entropy.

Innovation Boom and Market Chaos

Mass-market segment has attracted frugal innovation with low-cost and high-value proposition with the manifold growth of technology-led, start-up enterprises. The low-end markets are the consumer nucleus for commercializing reverse innovations and latter drive them to wider markets across geo-demographic agglomerations. The public policies also support start-up enterprises with financial resources to develop and market low-cost innovations in the niche markets. Consequently, competition in the frugal innovation segment has grown inordinately, causing chaos of low-cost consumer products, which have collectively cannibalized the regional and global brands in the mass consumer markets. Frugal innovation has improved (rather than decreased) the performance of the products deliverables in the low-end markets, despite extreme budget constraints. Such products have exhibited extensive designs and applied technological knowledge among consumers though social networks and digital media. The growing awareness on cost effectiveness and value for money among the consumers has helped them to adapt to frugal designs of innovative products. However, marketing of such products is relatively complex in the higher-price segment products such as automobiles and consumer durables (Lim and Fujimoto 2019).

Most companies play a proactive role to launch innovative products and prepare marketing strategies in reference to the existing market competition and business goals of the firms. Often, new products do not meet the desired success due to the lack of organizational policies and teamwork. Thus, it is required to inculcate team behavior in developing new products and popularizing them in the test market segments. The results of the test markets may be further carried out in the larger segments. It is essential to stimulate adequate brainstorming to map the basic (consumers' perceptions) and secondary (operational market players such as distributors, retailers, inventory managers, and the like) market requirements for the product, listing the product attributes, and identifying the forced relationship of other goods and services with the new product. Frugal innovations today are considered as technological product innovation for the low-end markets (mass- and lower-mass-market segment). Such innovations are linked to *design-to-market* strategies and help in attracting new consumers within niche market segments. In the social and economic context, frugal innovation can be explained as a technological movement to improve the performance of relatively complex products through cost-effective architectural changes and creation of community knowledge on user-friendly technology products. The domain of innovation policies and strategies activates frugal innovations and envelops integrative and strategic approaches in the low-end markets. The concept and approach of low-cost product design for low-income markets is not a recent start. For example, the concept of low-cost vehicles (and its concrete application in *Asian cars* in the Philippines and Indonesia) has existed since the 1970s. However, the market today is experiencing exceeding competition with marginal changes in the innovation with use values causing chaos and entropy of established markets (Govindarajan and Trimble 2012).

An innovation value chain comprises critical activities such as idea generation, conversion, and diffusion. Innovation is a process that embeds collecting new ideas from inside and outside the firm, screening and selecting ideas, funding them, and promoting and diffusing them companywide. Using this framework, managers get an end-to-end view of their innovation efforts. Accordingly, the weakest links can be identified, and innovation best practices can be tailored appropriately, to strengthen those links. It is important for the emerging firms to note that most innovations typically succumb to the aforementioned weak scenarios of an economically non-viable and technologically non-feasible idea, poor conversions between the ideation stage to the finished product stage in the innovation process, and feeble diffusion of innovations to the end users (Hansen and Birkinshaw 2007). Consumers in the mass, lower mass, and bottom-of-the-pyramid segments of developing economies are not able to afford the high-technology and high-price products despite rising incomes. These consumers suffer from additional constraints, such as poor public and private infrastructures or limited availability of services. Companies offering solutions by means of frugal innovations to the low-end market segment consumers build inclusive markets over time and contribute to the socio-economic development (Zeschky et al. 2014).

The pivotal role of creativity in organizations has been widely recognized by the academic community. Creativity is associated with the part of the innovation process, which is labeled as idea generation (Coyne et al. 2007). The ideation process for new product development can be stimulated through metaphors, pictures, and experience. It is rooted in the philosophy of rationalism and empiricism, implying "the truth is out there" approaches. It is observed that defining cognitive idea generation is based on personal experiences and beliefs driven by individual and social information. However, these forms of idea generation process are individualistic and not amenable to team contexts (Bhatt 2000). Frugal innovation is one of the major drivers of industrial growth, as it not only offers low-cost product architectures, but also connects the local companies managing frugal innovations with the large companies. Such innovations drive inclusive growth of companies and innovation portfolios within the industry and open up the low-end market segments and virtual domain of innovation in both emerging and advanced countries (innovation for low-income people). The digital domains of frugal innovations attract crowdsourcing of ideas and explore low-cost market infrastructure like online retailing, cloud-based supply chains, social media-led communications, and reaching out markets through psychodynamics. Frugal innovations, therefore, play a significant role in promoting contemporary industrial growth (Hart and Christensen 2002). There is typically an indirect connection between investment in research, innovation, and commercial benefit. Research is more likely to help generating ideas through the available information and public resources. More significantly, as discoveries are likely to be in the form of laws of nature, abstract ideas, and physical phenomena, they are likely to be converged with the end-user values and market potential from the perspective of business firms (Abernathy and Utterback 1978).

Frugal innovations are often considered as low-end market disruptors in emerging markets. Disruptive innovation refers to altered product designs that challenge incumbent firms to co-exist and compete in the marketplace. Changes in product attributes are perceived by consumers and companies as cognitive barriers to maintain the underlying value networks. Products and services with ease of use, affordability, and limited features are delivered to customers at the lower-end markets. The disruptive innovation, sometimes, caters to the latent needs of consumers at the niche markets (Hart and Christensen 2002). Successful innovation of new products leads to customer engagement and profits. Some companies have tried investing intensively in research and development. For many companies, developing new products is a *hit-or-miss the market task*, but successful innovation is not magical. It comes from careful attention to a small number of important criteria. The key concern is not the amount of money a company can spend, but the ways to spend money in the innovation process. The return on innovation investment concept correlates directly with organic growth and links innovation spending with financial performance in ways that can lead decision makers to generate higher, more reliable returns on innovation, and research and development. To become more effective, a company needs to diagnose its innovation practices and capabilities (Kandybin 2009).

Successful innovations emerge out of an idiosyncratic and systematic chain of action through analyzing causes and effects and intermittent feedbacks on concepts and applications that lead to *design-to-market products* or services. The trial and errors in positioning innovations are usually carried out by the enterprises with potential markets, consumer segments, and prototype testing routines. Companies that test innovative products and services in larger markets than niche might create wider demand, but over time, fragment to niche market segment as disruptive products emerge. Disruptive products create their own ecosystem comprising technology, suppliers, service providers, retailers, user networks, consumers, value streams, basic marketing-mix, industry attractiveness, and product and user lifecycles (Caraca, Ferreira, and Mendonca 2007).

Innovation boom in consumer-centric and industrial products has emerged after manufacturing technology and information technology have been fully explored and exploited in the big emerging markets like India and China. Innovation boom in emerging markets dates back to 1980s, which has spread across countries over the years through product attractiveness and price competition. The drivers of innovation boom and reasons for chaos and market fragmentation are illustrated in Figure 3.1. Innovation boom is broadly observed in the consumer and industrial products segments. In addition, social innovation in the health and family well-being, education, and services like retailing have rose into prominence over the years. Innovation boom has been driven by the growing innovations at the bottom-of-the-pyramid market segment, reverse innovations, and increasing disruptive innovations. Innovations at the grassroots of the market are based on low-cost and high-consumer surplus business philosophy and are widely driven by the socio-cultural needs, which embed potential demand. Frugal innovations use local resources, but exhibit potential for upstream entrepreneurship. Such innovations demonstrate high utilitarian values with higher rate of affordability and adaptability. Frugal innovations stay localized in niche markets and attract competition in the product market segment, causing slow growth in business and chaos in the niche.

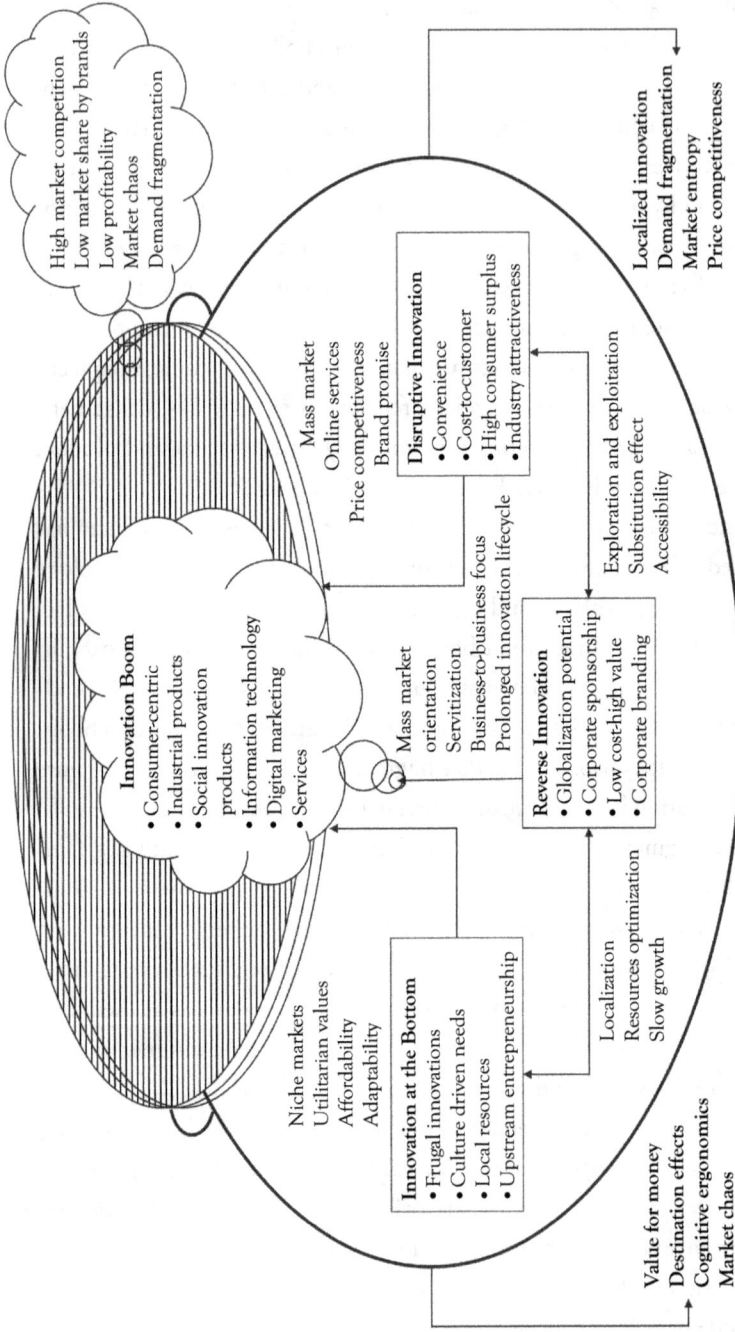

Figure 3.1 Innovation boom: Causes and effects

Source: Author

Reverse innovations are low-cost, price-competitive, and show business expansion potential. Large companies tend to sponsor reverse innovation products that have potential in global markets and serve the mass market. Reverse innovations are focused on the business-to-business segment and supported with the product services. Figure 3.1 illustrates that not only frugal and reverse innovations drive chaos in the market, but disruptive innovations also contribute to the market chaos and fragmentation. Disruptive innovations are developed and positioned in the market with a view to provide convenience to consumers and value for money. These innovations have high industry attractiveness comprising high frequency of new entrants and high substitution effect, causing chaos in the marketplace. Online services, price competitiveness, and brand promise of competing products also contribute to the chaotic situation in the marketplace. In view of the above discussion, it may be argued that innovation boom has been contributed by the emergence of frugal, reverse, and disruptive innovations. Innovation boom has caused high competition, industry rivalry, and chaos in the market. Consequently, high competition causes market entropy, demand fragmentation, consumer defection, and confinement to niche markets.

Commodity boom had turned the markets of developed economies during the mid-20th century, which bounced back on emerging markets with a new business philosophy entwined with radical innovations and marketing strategies. Frugal innovations had boomed in India and China since 1980s and spread across the consumer product portfolios in international markets. Between the early 1990s and 2014, the Latin American market has been characterized by positive economic performance, macroeconomic stability, and increasing visibility in the media that encouraged innovations to boom in niche markets. Low-cost innovations over the years have caused market chaos in the global marketplace by cannibalizing the market share of large companies. Such business scenario has caused fragmentation of demand and frequent defection of consumers across the multinational brands. The potential impact of consumption externalities has appeared on consumption surplus with low-cost innovation products of emerging markets (Dupor and Liu 2003).

Innovation lifecycle moves through stages of introduction, growth, maturity, and decline in the context of market behavior. However, the attributes of innovation cycle in different stages vary from the product or organization lifecycles to some extent. An innovation cycle cannot be determined in general, as there are various types of innovation and growth models in different market conditions. Innovation drivers in reference to its backward and forward linkages, unique propositions, innovation values, and high investment to carry out product innovation occur during the introduction stage of the innovation lifecycle. Firms foster the strategy of 4As to strengthen the product awareness, acceptance, availability, and affordability in order to reduce the market risk and gain competitive advantage of the new product in the marketplace. The lifecycles of frugal innovations are shorter and are not incremental. However, such innovations are spatially distributed and are developed across various product portfolios. Commercialization of frugal innovations triggers high competition in the marketplace over time and causes chaos. Innovations in the niche market are susceptible to temporal complexities. The frugal innovation has, thus, entered the spotlight of marketing management, raising questions on the emerging competitive models (Huang and Lai 2016).

Most companies tend to follow incremental innovation strategies, as they are cost-effective and easy to manage, by carrying out marginal augmentation in the existing attributes. Incremental innovations include simple product improvements or extensions of product line that marginally improve the existing performance of a product or service. By contrast, breakthrough innovations are carried out with new technology that contributes to substantial changes in their performance to enhance customer benefits as compared to existing products. These products lead to considerable changes and induce new consumption patterns among consumers (De Visser et al. 2010). Breakthrough innovation in a market is a continuous process that is backed by the distribution, retailing, and services industries. Innovations leading to commercial breakthroughs demonstrate a highly skewed distribution of use value of inventions: some are useless, a few are of moderate value, and there is rarely one that qualifies as a breakthrough. Those breakthroughs embed the long tail of innovation, and distribution plays a key role in the breakthrough process. It is necessary for a firm to account for the total number of inventions it generates and the average score out of the mean value of those inventions and to count the number of successful breakthrough inventions.

Such corporate awareness may help in developing strategic balance between individual innovation workers and teams. Firms develop dynamic innovation capabilities over time by accumulating their experience in radical, frugal, or incremental innovation. Local firms also develop abilities to exploit the existing resources. The accumulation of innovation expertise enables firms to get acquainted with the values associated with new innovations (Christensen et al. 2005).

Breakthrough innovations are driven by the market-oriented capabilities of the companies comprising leadership philosophy, competitor orientation, and functional coordination across geo-demographic segments. Breakthrough innovations are branded as technological innovation, which involve convergence of new technological knowledge and values associated with the end-user products. The high-quality technical innovations tend to replace inferior alternatives and help to increase the end-user value (Ulaga and Eggert 2006). Most innovation breakthroughs are market-oriented, which are derived from the existing, latent, or projected demand of consumer, to serve the existing market segment or new customers in new markets (Benner and Tushman 2003). Greater team diversity stimulates higher involvement in working with breakthrough innovations. Thus, it is the first and foremost requirement for the companies to introspect within the organization and identify how they want to improve their innovation process; take appropriate measures to drive the innovative products and services as breakthrough; and contrary to that, address any deficiencies in the process. Such dynamism in the innovation process allows the companies to improve their competencies and capabilities to innovate in ways that make the best sense for the organization and the market (Fleming 2007).

Breakthrough product innovations are central to the growth and transformation of markets and organizations. However, low-end markets tend to emulate the breakthrough products over time and fragment the demand for the products of high-price segments. The low-price product, along with the counterfeit products in the low-end market segments, drives chaos in the market over time. These products influence the up-market consumers considerably and drive large companies to develop low-end marketing strategies. For example, the growth of generic interchange (GI) pharmaceutical products that are price-sensitive and attract large number of consumers in the emerging markets and cannibalized a significant market share of commercial brands of large companies. Over time, the local pharmacies developed their own GI brands and the competition of GI products increased manifold within the niche market. Consequently, market for GI brands turned chaotic, which fragmented the demand and increased the frequency of customer defections across the GI brands. To compete with the price competition of GI brands, large companies launched low-end brands in the market. Such market phenomenon explains the causes and effects of market entropy. Pfizer, a leading pharmaceutical company, had to launch low-end brand product, Eturion (Atorvastain), under brand umbrella of *Vitales* in Mexico by fragmenting its market for high-end product Lipitor comprising identical compound, to match the price competition with GI products.

Market entropy drives companies to continuously explore low-end innovations and exploit existing markets safeguarding their brands against the fragmenting demand. Frugal innovations are challenging for large companies due to two processes: brand value trade-offs and the costs and benefits of low-end brands on macro perspectives, which change their marketing systems. Exploration of low-end markets are risk-averse, and the returns are distant and diffuse for large companies, though it helps in expanding business at the bottom-of-the-pyramid market segment (Cohen and Caner 2016).

Incremental Innovation

Longitudinal approach of reinforcing existing innovations with marginally augmenting values to predetermined consumer segments in a given market may be defined as incremental innovation. Introducing improvements in existing innovations over time is a common approach of firms to strengthen brand attractiveness and performance in a prevailing market. Incremental innovations are often induced through consumer participations and co-creation practices in the consumer-centric companies. Most companies at the bottom of the pyramid might not be able to engage in incremental innovations due to resource constraints. Therefore, these companies explore the possibilities of transferring the seed innovations to large companies at a negotiated innovation fee. Start-up and small enterprises are skeptical about getting their innovations patented due to the possibilities of whistleblowing and cumbersome administrative process. Consequently, these companies cannot negotiate with large companies on legal acquisition of innovations over the mutually preferred loyalty plans. In managing innovations at the low-end organizations, the flow of human capital and top-down knowledge significantly and positively influence both incremental and radical innovations. Social capital and bottom-up knowledge have a limited contribution in promoting periodical increments in frugal innovations. However, organizational capital could have a positive impact on desired incremental innovation over time (Nguyen 2018).

Incremental innovation can be integrated into the organization learning process with clear strategy and rightly placed and measured decision metrics, and management models like Stage-Gate create a working platform for all those involved in the innovation process. It is, thus, necessary to involve senior management of the firm to run the innovation process through the stage-gate paradigm and review the performance of activities at each stage to open the gate to carry innovation to the next stage. The innovation process is a teamwork, as it involves various functionaries to coordinate at different levels to let the innovative product into the market. Autocratic decision-making fails to engage all players in the product innovation process, including critical stakeholders, while a consensus not based on the rationale sinks every decision to its lowest possible effect. Incremental innovation can be administered through the following processes (Buffington and McCubbrey 2011):

- Innovation continuum can be established using a complex adaptive system.
- Incremental innovation is determined to possess adaptive qualities and can be enhanced using collaboration and dynamic business models.
- Discrete innovation is established as a creative process enabled through expert designers and improved through the use of generative design.

Frugal innovations are initiated by small teams in the start-up enterprises in the local markets across the consumer segments. An innovation process does not function without a leader who can make decisions and engage the team to support those decisions. Companies should develop cross-functional teams to drive steering of insights and mutual responsiveness in performing various operational tasks. The best teams have five critical dimensions that comprise warming, forming, storming, norming, and performing (Rajagopal 2008). Large companies encourage team innovations and drive coordinated efforts to bring breakthrough innovations in the marketplace. However, low-cost innovations targeted for the mass markets are carried out discretely in the start-up enterprises. These innovation teams serve as learning organizations, which tend to understand social needs, competitor moves, and business growth perspectives in an integrated way. In the technology- and consumer surplus-led business environment emphasizing various consumer touchpoints today, team innovation is increasingly critical to the market leadership of the companies. Large and niche markets drive the innovation continuum to gain strategic benefits for a firm. Putting the goal-setting theory into the input-process-output framework, the innovation process today is embedded in the business model to examine the relationship across consumerism, team innovation, and market competitiveness. China demonstrated that team innovation and business performance could establish the direct relationship between inclusive innovation and team voice as well as the consumer relationship between inclusive innovation and competitive advantages. It has been observed that the Chinese business environment has widely supported the philosophy of innovation continuum to generate long-term consumer surplus (Ye et al. 2019).

Teams should be capable of warming up topical discussions related to the product innovation, choose appropriate team members, allow brainstorming on the identified issues, set norms to refine the ideas and processes, and carry out the innovation process to perform in reference to the perspectives of the end users. Market dynamics and consumer preferences are volatile that govern the need for new products in the market. One of the major challenges for the companies in managing incremental innovations is to retain the supplier confidence and market demand. Vertical or incremental innovations are affected adversely if their brand name or extension differs from the previous brand, as consumers are often unable to relate them with their experience of previous brand and rebuild trust with the incremental version of the product. Consumer perceptions and values associated with the incremental innovation affect its performance. Companies not only offer value-added benefits to the customers, but also provide performance-based rewards to its employees to promote incremental innovation. Pay-for-performance has a stronger positive effect on radical innovation than on incremental innovation. Radical innovation may be achieved by rewarding suppliers for their performance only (Sumo et al. 2016). Successful companies develop a flexible attitude in product innovation and consider the changes in the market behavior while carrying out the innovation process. Marketplace factors, including customers, competition, government regulation, and science and technology, drive cultural change among the companies. Only by exploring these drivers of change, companies may realize what they must do to be relevant in its proposed product market planning (Govindrajan 2011). It is necessary for companies to develop customer-centric and social capabilities to explore appropriate geo-demographic consumer segments and markets to ensure full exploitation of radical and incremental innovations. In case of radical innovations, the exploration capabilities are enhanced by shared capabilities within the organization and in association with consumers (capability co-creation). Incremental innovation shows a positive influence toward exploitation capabilities and a concave relationship of exploration capabilities (Camison et al. 2018).

Incremental innovation is a common phenomenon in all types of consumer products ranging from toothpaste to an automobile. It is a process of continuous innovation over the existing products. Most firms prefer to engage in a series of small improvements to an existing product or product line that usually help in maintaining or improving their competitive position over time in the industry or against rivals. Incremental innovation is regularly used within the high-technology business by companies that need to continue to improve their products to include new features increasingly desired by consumers. However, radical innovation is about making major changes in existing products, taking them few stages ahead of the routine incremental innovation. A radical change can represent a radical innovation at a technological level, but the impact may show an incremental trend from an organizational perspective. The term *radical* often refers to the level of contribution made to the efficiency or revenue of the organization (McLaughlin et al. 2008). For example, by introducing flat screen televisions, manufacturers radically increased the demand for such products. Social needs and consumer behavior determine the need for incremental innovation and technological changes based on ethnic creativity and localized technical knowledge. Such symbiotic relations among the societal dynamics and innovations can be understood in terms of growth of knowledge and regional factors that co-define the incremental innovations. The technological and institutional attributes affect the progressive and existing pool of technological knowledge, which seed innovative ideas to grow in an affordable techno-economic environment (Ringberg et al. 2019).

Reverse Innovation and Marketing

Reverse innovation is commercially positioned by many large companies across the destinations to promote low-cost products in the global markets. However, why reverse innovation does not necessarily lead to the global brands and transfer to subsidiaries of large companies to gain significant profits remains as a pertinent question. Developing effective marketing and sales strategies in the appropriate market segments can help in transfer of reverse innovations to successfully contribute to the business performance. The parent innovation organization mediates the relationship between enterprise owning reverse innovation and acquiring company. However, the indirect relationship toward consumer behavior, societal needs, and geo-political business diplomacy is moderated by business culture specificity and inter-firm attributes and propensity to acquire the local innovations (Wang et al. 2019).

Deriving innovation ideas for mass customization and global marketing has become the current practice among innovation companies. Customer-centric innovations are largely developed by start-up enterprises analyzing the customer needs within the niche market. Most of the innovations positioned in the premier niche markets are of high quality and high cost, while innovations focused on the mass consumers in the local niche are of acceptable quality and deliver the value for money.

The two factors: cost and marketability, drive the strategy of reverse innovation. Large companies, thus, roll over to local markets to identify the customer-centric innovations developed by local enterprises and tend to evaluate the economics of their business projects. When a company with capability of sponsoring the reverse innovation investigates a new product opportunity, it not only defines the problem to which the innovation serves as a solution, but also lists the requirements that are needed for commercializing the innovation. The sponsoring companies then develop ways to deliver a viable solution for wider markets. Reverse innovation helps companies penetrate the emerging markets or create high-performance, high-value products and services at low cost and affordable prices that consumers with low per capita income find appealing. The primary challenge to developing innovations for emerging markets and catering to the customers therein is delivering solutions of adequate quality at a competitive price for the masses (Rajagopal 2016a).

Reverse innovation plays an important role in developing low-cost and utilitarian products for commercialization in the global markets. With the development of economic globalization, reverse innovation developed by the enterprises of the emerging markets has received increased attention in the customer-centric companies. Co-creation embedded with the value-driven factors leads the success of reverse innovation projects and generates considerable response among engineering and technical services enterprises. Locally grown technology, connection with international markets, and integration with industrial chain contribute to the success of reverse innovation in global markets. The small and medium enterprises nurturing reverse innovations pay full attention to gain comprehensive advantage in the niche markets and tend to stay price-competitive in the regional and global markets. The diversified international coupling mechanism is an important support for technology localization and developing business models for reverse innovation products and services. The engineering and technical service enterprises pay attention to the service chain of the vertical integration in the process of reverse innovation (Xu and Xu 2016).

The international innovation companies need to segment their markets as upstream and mass markets that fit into the innovation attributes such as the price, value for money, perceived value, performance, and product lifecycle. Companies may have to deliver high-performance products in western markets with high price, while reverse innovation offers the companies the opportunity to enter the emerging markets with the same corporate and extended brand strength. Determining the performance of technology is a commercial prerequisite. For example, in the case of generic two-wheeler motorbike engines, the performance of technology has to be measured in reference to emission reduction and longevity of engine life at the affordable price. It is one of the business parameters in creating products for emerging markets. Commercialization of reverse innovation often gives a radical push to the product, company, and industry. Commercializing reverse innovation is a disruptive leap to hit a product in the target market, and it demands organizational insight into how a new product could drive an impact in emerging market. A product that delivers significantly better performance at a lower price may become the basis for a new product platform, which can have features added or removed to adjust its price and performance to the specific needs of wealthy or poor markets, and makes the reverse innovation management a success.

The manufacturing sector is increasingly looking at innovation to ensure productivity growth, especially in low-cost operating environments, to achieve price competitiveness. As the global markets are reshaping rapidly in view of the consumers' changing purchasing power and buying propensity, the balance between price and quality determines the product and market attractiveness of reverse innovations. However, co-creation is critical to the reverse innovation, and its effective commercialization forms the basis for success. In addition, diffusion of reverse innovations in the context of both geo-demographic proximity and corporate branding predominantly strengthen the image of reverse innovations in the marketplace. The socio-economic context of such innovations helps companies diffuse their attributes globally and explore ways into developed markets (Hossain et al. 2016).

GE Healthcare has demonstrated this idea with the customization of its low-cost ultrasound and electrocardiogram machines, which started as emerging market products and then evolved into valuable devices for North America and Europe. Companies can envisage the process engineering map of reverse innovations before any prototypes are made.

Reverse innovation products move slowly during the adaptation process in the non-familiar consumer segments and face price constraints in the market. However, based on the existing technologies, companies can develop a business-linked manufacturing plan for reverse innovation to develop the product line by reviewing benchmarks of competing products in the marketplace. They can, thus, analyze the possibilities of outwitting, outperforming, and outmaneuvering competitors while delivering the low-cost and better performing solutions to consumers. By scoping onto the worldwide market opportunities, and by understanding the probable constraints in marketing the products across market segments and destinations, companies can engineer reverse innovations to mark impact on markets and consumers in the global marketplace (Winter and Govindarajan 2015, Rajagopal 2016a). The factors driving convergence of reverse and frugal innovations toward incremental innovation are illustrated in Figure 3.2.

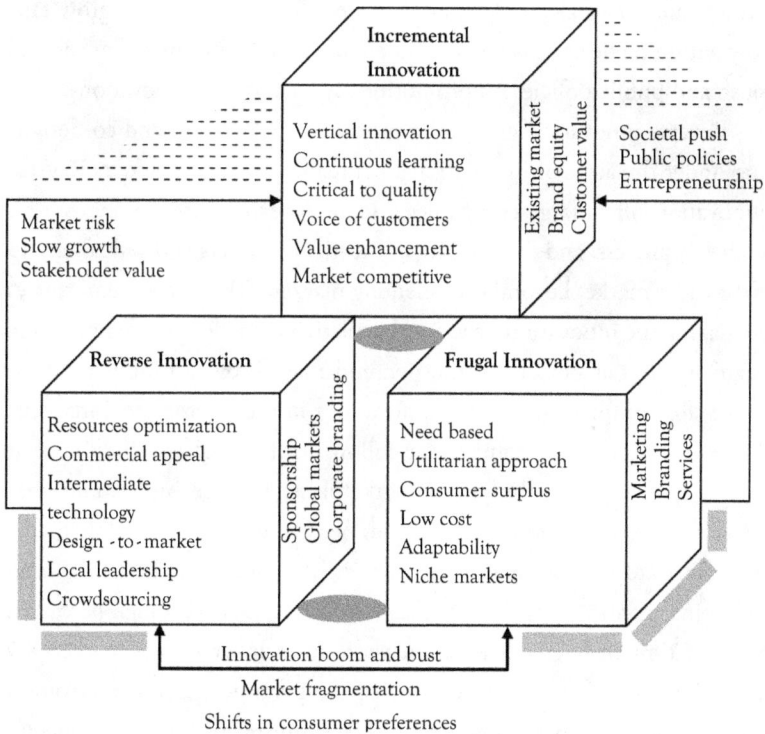

Figure 3.2 Convergence of innovations by taxonomy

Source: Author

Innovation boom is triggered by reverse and frugal innovations at the bottom of the pyramid. These innovations are need-based, tend to optimize resources, and exhibit commercial appeal, as illustrated in Figure 3.2. However, they stay in the niche market unless acquired by the large companies in view of their global marketing potential. As both types of innovation cater to the social needs, they grow in the market with the design-to-market approach. Entrepreneurs engaged in either type of innovation improve the existing attributes based on consumer feedback or crowdsourced ideas. Such strategy leads to vertical innovation through continuous learning and applying critical-to-quality parameters to the existing products. The incremental innovation enables the products to stay market competitive in the context of relative pricing, consumer surplus, corporate brand leverage, and customer value. Reverse innovations possess high market risk, as they are aimed at gaining faster market share and regional expansion. Consequently, reverse innovations have slow growth and low stakeholder value, whereas frugal innovations grow rapidly within niche and also benefit small innovation enterprises for societal push and public policies on promoting low-cost native innovations.

Reverse innovation grows as a process of co-creation and co-designing under the aegis of international companies in local markets. Reverse innovation offers large companies a scope to experience the innovation concept, process, and deliverables in the niche markets and scale them up for a wider market beyond the emerging markets. The start-up enterprises managing the innovation need for the relatively smaller geo-demographic segments and at bottom of the pyramid may throw up immense challenges for commercializing the innovations in the international markets. However, it requires a company to follow institutionalized thinking that guides its actions in the global marketplace. Reverse innovations that are adopted by the sponsor companies need to make design adjustments and fabricate for the mass consumers in the global markets in a radically simpler and cheaper way to serve the customer with high perceived value. Companies can develop new products in emerging markets by using a radical change from bottom of the pyramid (generic innovation design) combined with smart leadership from top (up-market strategy). The small start-up enterprises may set audacious goals to match with the new organizational structure of sponsors and adopt new design and commercialization methods. However, the start-up enterprises may also nurture the reverse innovation, provided they could arrange adequate resources to up-scale the innovation by shifting the gravity of business beyond emerging markets (Govindarajan 2012, Rajagopal 2016a).

The current demand for products in the overseas markets shows the business potential. It also warns about the intensive competition. Many companies are engaged in the market operations in international market, selling competitive products with marginal differentiation that trigger high substitution effect and increase the bargaining power of consumers in reference to price and promotion. One of the pro-company demand situations present in the markets is the latent demand when the demand for the products exists, but the products are not available. Companies can take advantage of markets in such destinations and enjoy near-monopoly for a short period as it takes time for the local competition to emerge. Companies can use this near-monopoly market situation to architect brand and set price levels and deliver adequate customer value to generate brand loyalty. Most companies exploiting the latent demand realize the first-mover advantages and attain market leadership. Companies engaged in manufacturing and marketing of high-technology and high-value products often need to create demand by educating the consumers on the prescribed and perceived use values of their products and services. Such demand situation is explained as an incipient demand. In an incipient demand, though companies enjoy the near-monopoly situation for a short period, the market share grows slowly, as most consumes respond slow to the experimental products. However, in both latent and incipient demand situations, there is threat of emergence of disruptive technology and products that target to attack the market share of these companies (Rajagopal 2016b).

Microeconomic factors are found within a company's business environment, and they guide the company in managing its competitiveness in the destination market. The microeconomic factors are largely woven around the marketing-mix followed by the company. Globalization has altered the conventional marketing-mix to a large extent, and now, the elements of marketing-mix possess 11Ps comprising the conventional 4Ps, including product, price, place, and promotion. In addition, 5Ps, including packaging, pace (competitive dynamics), people (front liners in marketing), performance, and psychodynamics (peer-to-peer, word or mouth, or the grapevine effect), constitute the extended operational factors of marketing-mix. The additional 2Ps known as corporate factors involve posture (corporate image) and proliferation (product and market diversification). This new marketing-mix concept has become an essential part of marketing practices of multinational companies. The integration of 11Ps in a marketing-mix strategy is both effective and simple. Interconnecting the marketing-mix elements such as product, price, packaging, and promotion with psychodynamics and posture, companies may gain sustainable competitive advantage like Samsung in the consumer electronics product markets and Wal-Mart in the global retailing sector. By applying marketing-mix, companies can attain consistency, integration, and leverage in a marketing program to fit the needs of the marketplace (Rajagopal 2011).

The fundamental drivers of reverse innovation are the disposable income of consumers, consumer culture, cost of innovation, and price of the deliverable to the end users. As the gaps in the innovation process widen across the elements of innovations, the innovative products tend to fall off the market soon that shortens the product lifecycle. There is no way to design a product for the American mass market and then simply adapt it for the Chinese or Indian mass market due the elements discussed earlier. Buyers in the emerging markets, who are price-sensitive, demand solutions on an entirely different price–performance curve and turn loyal to the brand if the innovative products satisfy the consumers, uphold the value for money, and offer competitive advantage. Consumers demand new, high-tech solutions that deliver at low costs and match with their personal standards of *good enough* quality. In fact, reverse innovation is not always a prolific solution for the large companies to boost their revenue and business growth. However, reverse innovation is the bottom-up outcome of what consumers look for, and hence, embeds enormous potential for mass marketing. As the Darwinian effect in market evolution is seen in the global marketplace, multinational companies are trying to uncover the remote niches of the mass market and bottom-of-the-pyramid market segments. On the contrary, local companies are seeking expansion. Reverse innovations will power the future of large companies (international) to reach consumers in the lesser-known markets. Hence, to stay noticed and sustain the market competition, multinational companies must adopt reverse innovation beyond their home market.[1] Successful and long-established multinational corporations, who are seeking explosive growth in emerging economies, must now learn new tricks of in order to succeed. Reverse innovation directs them how to make innovations successful in emerging markets and how such innovations can unlock opportunities throughout the world (Govindarajan and Trimble 2012).

Innovation Breakthrough Projects

Breakthrough innovations are essential for a company to sustain and renew opportunities for continuous business growth and corporate profitability. These innovations can be high price or frugal innovations. Breakthrough innovations in the mass market segment are measured by the utilitarian values and the consumer surplus delivered by the innovation. Supported by effective marketing strategies, these innovations advance with the state of the technology and create new order of the world products (Zhou and Li 2012).

Companies often explore innovation ideas either by activating the crowdsourcing tools, outside-the-box thinking, collecting information from the consumers in the existing market, and collecting financial data on innovations in reference to the cost and time. The major problem with the crowdsourcing of ideas is that few people are very good at unstructured and abstract brainstorming. It is difficult for the project teams to ensure as how crowdsourced ideas to fit into the canvas of economic viability, technological feasibility, marketability, product services, and customer value. The problems with the process of outside-the-box thinking are that databases are usually compiled to describe current market requirements and do not offer strategies for the next generation products. Hence, there are possibilities that customers rarely come forward to express whether they need or want a product they have never seen. Such situation triggers creating demand for the innovation, requires more resources for the project,

---

[1] Extracted for the Vijaya Govindarajan's blog http://tuck.dartmouth.edu/people/vg/blog-archive/2009/10/what_is_reverse_innovation.htm (accessed July, 2019).

and consumes longer time, which, at some point, may also be risk-averse, as competitors may penetrate the market with identical or similar products. Breakthrough innovations are outgrown from the local knowledge and needs (reverse innovation), which play a significant role in transforming the markets and organizations. Companies engaged in bringing up the breakthrough innovations continuously face the challenge of exploring the right consumer preferences and pose and surface customer-centric affordable innovations. Breakthrough innovations are supported by external knowledge. These innovations are governed by their lifecycle, and those that have a short lifecycle fragment into niche markets. Breakthrough innovations are also susceptible to market entropy in a span of their lifecycle. However, as the innovations fragment to niche markets level, exploring new consumer segments and reinforcing referred values are risky, and the returns are distant and diffuse (Gupta et al. 2006).

The secret of new innovations is to convert workable ideas into action and turn some great ones marketable. In doing so, it is necessary for the innovation companies to create new platforms for innovation players comprising consumers, trend gatekeepers, product critics, researchers, and employees of the company, who could generate new ideas in the context of knowledge, skills, and previous experience (Coyne et al. 2007). Most firms commit fewer resources during the innovation process, as they believe that innovations are risk-averse. Consequently, they tend to focus innovations in niche markets than taking them to up-market stream. Exploring the existing products with an incremental value, thus, gains higher priority than investing in breakthrough products and related innovations. Exploring consumer attributes and markets includes *experimentation with new alternatives*, while exploitation of market opportunities can be explained as the refinement of existing competencies, technologies, and business paradigms to serve innovations. The need for both exploration and exploitation within organizations is a well-defined business perspective that guides companies to work with new innovations (He and Wong 2004).

Sustaining an innovation is the key for a company's long-term success. However, successful innovations are not very frequent. The innovation projects need excellent analytical skills and should have the potential to identify the solutions to the consumer problems. Such approach of innovation projects suggests nurturing customer-centric innovations. The innovation projects are to be developed socially savvy to align with the consumers and markets. In managing reverse innovations, the right talent management procedures can help in spotting potential innovators. Developing breakthrough innovations requires appropriate mentoring and involvement of peer networks. Mentors provide motivations, set goals, develop entrepreneurial mindset, and resolve budget constraints in reference to the new product development or innovation projects. Peer networks provide a sense of solidarity and a uniquely fertile environment in which to exchange ideas, impart information, and instill hope among the members of the innovation project teams (Cohn et al. 2008).

The social and customer-centric innovations are converted over time to breakthrough innovations upon realizing its customer value and market behavior. Companies managing such innovative business projects reach beyond familiar domains and strive for divergent ideas, using widely crowdsourced and co-created ideas. However, some firms like IKEA tend to act conservatively in selecting different novel ideas and develop them with design-to-market strategies. This process tends to bring unfamiliar technologies to the market, measure their marketing potential, and create value among customers. Such innovations are perceived as innovation at the bottom of the pyramid that have a potential to be successful in the marketplace. Such innovations in the global markets furnish reliable estimates of economic gain and can be commercialized via familiar business models through a customer-centric model, which explains marketing of products from large markets to niche environment (Cohen and Caner 2016).

The Internet and the open innovation have significantly encouraged new ideas and solutions to spur in the market for consumer convenience and satisfaction, and business performance of companies. The main challenge in managing innovation projects is toward taking advantage of the growing technology and developing convergence with the innovation business project. Innovation-led products in the marketplace should gain the first-mover advantage to survive the competition. A large body of new knowledge and efforts to discovery drives advancements to existing knowledge and helps firms to reorient them on breakthrough innovations. Besides invention, new ideas grow with frugal innovations and proceed through continuous cycles of commercialization in which design ideas are drafted, tested, and refined. Mass-market innovations that incorporate new technologies or address unfamiliar needs present social challenge to companies toward generating awareness, attributes, affordability, and adaptability (Bessant et al. 2010).

Most companies focus on employing new technologies to better serve the customers' existing needs, while others strive to create products and services that can provide the customers with a completely new reason to buy a product as innovative and unique. For example, Nintendo, with the Wii; Apple, with the iPod; and Swatch, with its fashionable and affordable watches, provide the rationale of *innovation to market* (Verganti 2011). Commonly, the breakthroughs constitute the *long tail* of innovation. To launch successful breakthrough, companies need to consider the total number of inventions a company develops in a financial year for different markets, average performance of inventions in the markets in terms of market share and profit contribution of innovative products, and the rate of success of breakthrough inventions can be measured through the customer values. Various factors that affect the deliverables of an innovation project include innovation alliances with other companies, the innovation team, diversity, and the degree of customization of the product to suit the consumer needs (Fleming 2007).

Market innovations are grown on the product concept that offers high customer surplus and utilitarian values over the conventional products. Market innovation is competition-oriented, and companies that aim to leading the oligopolistic market opt for investing in such innovations. Innovations of this kind carry instable lifecycle, as their performance is driven by the attributes of competition. This suggests that to create value, companies need to develop innovation to serve as solutions co-created with the consumers. The value creation in terms of both technological innovation and market-driven innovation needs to involve stakeholders and consumers to match with their expectations. Market innovations, thus, lead to short- and long-term performance in the market with a varied span of lifecycles. Technological innovation has a positive impact on the economic and strategic export performance of firms. In less-competitive markets, the positive relationship between technological innovations becomes even stronger indicator for commercializing social and break-through innovations (Silva et al. 2017).

Most companies expect their product development teams to create breakthroughs in reference to new products that can allow the innovative products to grow rapidly in the target markets and maintain high market share, leading to higher profit contribution. The involvement of project teams in breakthroughs is expensive and time consuming. However, product line extensions can help the bottom line immediately to position an incremental innovation over the existing product. It has been observed that innovators are often not efficient marketers to achieve breakthroughs, and it is required that innovation teams educate the marketing teams on innovation-led products meticulously and educate them on product attributes, technology, lifecycle, functionality, and serviceability. By the mid-1990s, lack of such a system was a problem even for an innovative company like 3M. Then, a project team in 3M's Medical-Surgical Markets Division became acquainted with a method for developing break-through products: the lead user process. The process is based on the fact that many commercially important products are initially thought of, and even prototyped by *lead users*—the companies, organizations, or individuals who are well ahead of market trends. Their needs are so far beyond those of the average user that lead users create innovations on their own that may later contribute to commercially attractive breakthroughs. The lead-user process transforms the job of inventing breakthroughs into a systematic task of identifying lead users and learning from them (von Hippel et al. 1999). Another example is the process of innovative new projects at General Electric (GE) Company to market as breakthrough innovation that would serve as the centerpiece of GE's organic growth initiative. The breakthrough process follows the company, as these changes are driven through the business units, focusing on GE Transportation, as it launches a series of groundbreaking, green products from the Evolution Locomotive to the Hybrid Locomotive. The growth process transforms the culture within GE Transportation, leading to a redefinition of the marketing role, the implementation of a *growth leader* profile and new decision-making processes to encourage innovation and risk (Bartlet et al. 2007).

Diffusion and Adaptation of Innovations

The diffusion and adaptation of new innovations have social, economic, and personal challenges among consumers. Thus, implementation of innovation is a complex process, which not only involves generating awareness and comprehension among the stakeholders and consumers, but also needs to meet the socio-economic and cultural criteria. The community-driven marketplaces like ethnic and bottom-of-the pyramid destinations offer innovations with culturally embedded use values and buying behavior. Unlike the technology-led innovative products of large companies, reverse and radical innovation products show most pressing challenges. However, there are a range of stakeholders in marketing innovative products and barriers, which can potentially impede and hinder the diffusion of innovation in the consumer products segment. Successful companies rely on a systematic innovation diffusion approach and map drivers and barriers to the diffusion and adaptation of innovation. These companies also identify stakeholders, affecting diffusion and adaptation processes within the specific context of the market and industry (Gruenhagen and Parker 2020).

Since the mid-20th century, innovation and technology have been growing faster than the diffusion of information on innovation and technology. As diffusion of innovation and technology is slower than their growth, the performance of innovation and technology-led products have initial low market share and slow growth of sales. Therefore, their breakeven point (BEP) is delayed, affecting their contribution to profit. Hence, companies should develop suitable consumer education and demonstration policies for innovative products before or during the early launch period to disseminate competitive advantages with unique selling proposition. Innovation companies partner with other enterprises to diffuse innovations and consumer communication, including social media communication, advertising, and interactive learning projects like do-it-yourself activities, in-store demonstrations, one-on-one communication with consumers, and telemarketing.

Often, high-technology high-value innovations lead to conspicuous consumption and are positioned in the premium niche. Such innovations have relatively lower consumer surplus, but carry higher social status than the innovations positioned in the mass consumer segment. They reach an early BEP as compared to the innovations in mass markets. However, the lifecycles of conspicuous innovative products are lower than the utilitarian innovation products of the mass consumer segment. The consumer perceptions of luxury and social status affect the technology-led innovative products in the market. For example, consumer perceptions of luxury, or necessity for a relatively novel technology associated with an electric vehicle, determines its market potential. The marketing theories explain such complex notion of conspicuous consumption and diffusion of innovation. In view of the neo-classical, theoretical variations on adaptation, consumption, and diffusion of innovation, a new logical congruence can be proposed as conspicuous diffusion of innovations. This converges conspicuous consumption effects with technological and societal development and explains how diffusion of innovation is intrinsically connected to status (Noel et al. 2019).

The company–consumer interlocking through effecting diffusion strategies of innovative products works efficiently through the interpersonal communication on social networks and direct marketing approaches. Firms can use social networks to build relationships with co-creative business partners and understand emerging threats in new competitive environments. Such relationship ties between companies and customers help to drive the consistency in consumption of innovative products. However, companies should identify the key barriers that prevent networks for discontinuous innovation and present specific strategies that can stimulate the adaptation process for new products. In order to build synergy among the growth of innovation and technology approaches, and diffusion of innovation strategies, companies may face various challenges, including finding the right partners to engage with, forming relationships with consumers, and then building high-performing innovation dissemination networks (Birkinshaw et al. 2007).

Self-referred and self-induced innovations grow within innovator communities. Such innovations are initially frugal in nature and turn as reverse innovation when acquired by the large companies for commercialization. The innovator communities are small and socially structured, and they grow in a makerspace. These creative groups are open communities for tinkering, innovating, and socializing, which are equipped with ideas and training tools that support creativity toward crafting innovations. It has been argued that makerspace can be a powerful vehicle to enhance both innovation and innovation diffusion by consumers. Most entrepreneurs, who are motivated to innovate and diffuse their innovation, tend to join makerspaces to exploit the rich knowledge-based and tangible community resources. Makerspaces tend to improve the opportunities to innovate and diffuse successfully. As innovation by consumers is both personally and economically valuable, makerspaces appear to be a valuable public investment (Halbinger 2018).

Traditional approaches to innovation strategy of both start-up enterprises and large companies assume that the world is relatively stable and predictable. But globalization, new technologies, and greater transparency combined together overturn the business environment. Such shift in the business environment has generated more risk and vulnerability among companies in engaging with new innovative projects. Hence, managers are finding an increasing need to develop organizational capabilities to foster competitive advantage rapidly for encouraging adaptation to innovations among consumers. Instead of frequently innovating a new product that could overlap with the previous products of the company launched in the short span, they should explore prospective innovation partners who could take the responsibility of developing and implementing the consumer information strategies. Companies should also be good at learning how to co-create new things by earning the confidence of market players like business partners, distributors, retailers, and consumers. Companies that thrive to follow the integrated innovation strategies as discussed earlier can quickly alter the consumer behavior and manage the market demand. In order to achieve a sustainable market for innovative product, companies need to experiment frequently not only with products and services, but also with business models, processes, and strategies. It is also necessary for the innovation-driven companies to acquire skills to manage complex multi-stakeholder systems in an increasingly interconnected world of consumers (Reeves and Deimler 2011).

Large innovation-led companies associating their innovation process with the start-up enterprises serve customers through a broad array of interfaces, from retail sales customer relations team to e-commerce teams, managing voice-response telephone systems to educate consumers on innovations as well as to resolve their problems. Typically, companies believe in investing in various consumer interface tools, but might not use any impressive interface collections due to a weak interface system that requires upgrading the skills of employees managing such interfaces. Most companies have the impression that smaller set of people and too many machines operating with insufficient coordination tend to increase complexity, costs, and customer dissatisfaction. Such corporate beliefs are found to be wrong with the experience of automobile companies, as the employees work with clear division of labor despite the plant and process automation. In a world where companies compete not on what they sell but on how they sell it, they could easily establish their innovation, brand, services, and customer relations despite the odds in market competition (Rayport and Jaworski 2004).

The process of innovation, diffusion, and adaptation of innovations to markets largely depends on the leadership embedded in the company. Transformational leadership is associated with organizational innovation, which supports new ways of innovation diffusion and develops organizational strategies to promote adaptation of the innovation. Transformational leadership style emphasizes the consciousness of collective interest among members of the organization to converge with the customer and market requirements. A pro-customer and pro-market leadership helps companies achieve their goals in diffusing innovations and driving their adaptation by integrating customers, marketers, and society. It provides a favorable market environment for innovation by co-creating an ambidextrous value system between organizations and markets. Transformational leadership helps in raising the motivation levels to bridge the gap between deliveries of innovation, training, and building its utilitarian values. Employee engagement in diffusion of the innovation process with an objective to stimulate need, creativity, and preferences influences the *design-to-market* and *critical-to-quality* systems in commercializing innovations. Breakthrough innovations are widely supported by the leadership patterns to succeed in the marketplace (Nguyen et al. 2017).

The new product attractiveness may comprise product features including improved attributes, use of advance technology, innovativeness, extended product applications, brand augmentation, perceived use value, competitive advantages, corporate image, product advertisements, and sales and services policies associated therewith. All these features contribute in building sustainable customer values toward making buying decisions on the new products. The introduction of new technological products makes it important for marketers to understand how innovators or first adopters respond to persuasion cues. It has been observed in a study that the innovativeness and perceived product newness, two of the many constituents of new product attractiveness, are independent constructs that have independent effects on a customer's attitude toward the brand and purchase intent for the new product. The attractiveness of new products is one of the key factors affecting the decision making of customers and is, in turn, related to market growth and sales. The higher the positive reactions of the customers toward the new products in view of their attractiveness, the higher the growth in sales and in market (Lafferty and Goldsmith 2004).

Most customers resist adapting to the new products, which hinders the performance and growth of new and innovative products in the marketplace. Therefore, companies launching new products should develop comprehensive innovation diffusion plan, including do-it-yourself product demonstration, product advertisements, and communication on the social media, in order to develop product attractiveness and confidence in consumers to adapt to the new products. To manage innovation in a systematic way, it is important for the companies to define innovation and its marketing prospects that would give them real feel about the innovation, and they could calculate its payoffs over the period. Developing *applied innovation* is harder than the *concept innovation*, products as the product derived from applied innovation stay beyond the popular conventions of consumerism and lack in innovativeness that stimulates the consumers. Cosmetic innovation, such as packaging ketchup in a new squeeze bottle, is neither a new nor incremental innovation. However, some marketing strategies that push innovation with value additions could make the innovative products move in the market along with the competitive products.

Summary

Frugal innovation today is considered as a technological product innovation for the low-end markets (mass and lower-mass-market segment).

Such innovations are linked to *design-to-market* strategies and help in attracting new consumers within niche market segments. An innovation value chain comprises idea generation, conversion, and diffusion as the critical activities. Innovation is a process that includes evaluating new ideas from inside and outside the firm, screening and selecting ideas, funding them, and promoting and diffusing them in markets. Using this framework, managers get an end-to-end view of their innovation efforts. Frugal innovations are often considered as low-end market disruptors in emerging markets. Disruptive innovation refers to altered product designs that challenge incumbent firms to co-exist and compete in the marketplace. Innovation lifecycle moves through a common lifecycle comprising introduction, growth, maturity, and decline in the context of market behavior. Firms foster the strategy of 4As to strengthen the product awareness, acceptance, availability, and affordability in order to reduce the market risk and gain competitive advantage of the new product in the marketplace.

Incremental innovation can be integrated into the organization learning process with clear strategy and rightly placed and measured decision metrics. Management models like Stage-Gate create a working platform for all those involved in the innovation process. Vertical or incremental innovations are affected adversely if the brand name or extension differs to the previous brand, as consumers are often unable to relate with their experiences of previous brand and rebuild trust with the incremental version of the product. Reverse innovation is commercially recognized by many large companies across destinations to promote low-cost products in the global markets. Reverse innovation plays an important role in developing low-cost and utilitarian products for commercialization in the global markets. Commercializing reverse innovation is a disruptive leap to hit a product in the target market, and it demands to develop an organizational insight into how a new product could drive an impact in an emerging market.

Reverse innovation is commercially regarded by many large companies to promote low-cost products in the global markets. Reverse innovation plays an important role in developing low-cost and utilitarian products for commercialization in the global markets. Commercializing reverse innovation is a disruptive leap to hit a product in the target market, and it demands to develop an organizational insight into how a new product could drive an impact in emerging market. The fundamental driver of reverse innovation is the disposable income of consumers, consumer culture, cost of innovation, and the price of deliverable to the end users.

Companies engaged in bringing up the breakthrough innovations continuously face the challenge of exploring the right consumer preferences in terms of innovation attributes and associated values. Market innovations are grown on the product concept that offers high customer surplus and utilitarian values over the conventional products. The diffusion and adaptation of innovations have social, economic, and personal challenges among consumers.

References

Abernathy, W.J., and J.M. Utterback. 1978. "Patterns of Innovation in Industry." *Technology Review* 80, pp. 40–47.

Benner, M.J., and M.L. Tushman. 2003. "Exploitation, Exploration, and Process Management: The Productivity Dilemma Revisited." *Academy of Management Review* 28, pp. 238–56.

Bessant, J., B. Von Stamm, K.M. Moeslein, and A.N. Neyer. 2010. "Backing Outsiders: Selection Strategies for Discontinuous Innovation." *R & D Management* 40, pp. 345–56.

Bhatt, G. 2000. "Organising Knowledge in the Knowledge Development Cycle." *Journal of Knowledge Management* 4, pp. 15–26.

Birkinshaw, J., J. Bessant, and R. Delbridge. 2007. "Finding, Forming, and Performing: Creating Networks for Discontinuous Innovation." *California Management Review* 49, pp. 67–83.

Buffington, J., and D. McCubbrey. 2011. "A Conceptual Framework of Generative Customization as an Approach to Product Innovation and Fulfillment." *European Journal of Innovation Management* 14, pp. 388–403.

Camisón, C., M. Boronat-Navarro, and B. Forés. 2018. "The Interplay Between Firms'" Internal and External Capabilities in Exploration and Exploitation." *Management Decision* 56, pp. 1559–80.

Caraça, J., J. Ferreira, and S. Mendonça. 2007. "A Chain-Interactive Innovation Model for the Learning Economy: Prelude for a Proposal." In *Working Paper 2007/12*. Lisbon: Department of Economics. ISEG.

Cohen, S.K., and T. Caner. 2016. "Converting Inventions into Breakthrough Innovations: The Role of Exploitation and Alliance Network Knowledge Heterogeneity." *Journal of Engineering and Technology Management* 40, pp. 29–44.

Coyne, K.P., P.G. Clifford, and R. Dye. 2007. "Breakthrough Thinking from inside the Box." *Harvard Business Review* 85, pp. 70–83.

Christensen, M.C., S. Cook, and T. Hall. 2005. "Marketing Malpractice." *Harvard Business Review* 83, pp. 74–83.

De Visser, M., P. Weerd Nederhof, D. Faems, M. Song, B. Van Looy, and K. Visscher. 2010. "Structural Ambidexterity in NPD Processes: A Firm level Assessment of the Impact of Differentiated Structures on Innovation Performance." *Technovation* 30, pp. 291–99.

Dupor, W., and W. Liu. 2003. "Jealousy and Equilibrium Overconsumption." *American Economic Review* 93, pp. 423–28.

Fleming, L. 2007. Breakthroughs and the Long Tail of Innovation. *MIT Sloan Management Review* 49, no. 1, pp. 69–74.

Govindrajan, V. 2011. "Innovation's Nine Critical Success Factors." *HBR Blog Network*, http://blogs.hbr.org/govindarajan/2011/07/innovations-9-critical-success.html

Govindarajan, V., and C. Trimble. 2012. *Reverse Innovation: Create Far from Home, Win Everywhere*. Boston, MA: Harvard Business Review Press.

Gruenhagen, J.H., and R. Parker. 2020. "Factors Driving or Impeding the Diffusion and Adoption of Innovation in Mining: A Systematic Review of the Literature." *Resources Policy* 65, Art. 101540.

Gupta, A.K., K.G. Smith, and C.E. Shalley. 2006. "The Interplay Between Exploration and Exploitation." *Academy of Management Journal* 49, pp. 693–706.

Halbinger, M.A. 2018. "The Role of Makerspaces in Supporting Consumer Innovation and Diffusion: An Empirical Analysis." *Research Policy* 47, pp. 2028–36.

Hansen, M.T., and J. Birkinshaw. 2007. "The Innovation Value Chain." *Harvard Business Review* 85, pp. 121–30, 142.

Hart, S.L., and C.M Christensen. 2002. "The Great Leap." *MIT Sloan Management Review* 44, pp. 51–56.

He, Z.L., and P.K. Wong. 2004. "Exploration vs. Exploitation: An Empirical Test of the Ambidexterity Hypothesis." *Organization Science* 15, pp. 487–94.

Hossain, M., H. Simula, and M Halme. 2016. "Can Frugal Go Global? Diffusion Patterns of Frugal Innovations." *Technology in Society* 46, pp. 132–39.

Hung, S.C., and J.Y. Lai. 2016. "When Innovations Meet Chaos: Analyzing the Technology Development of Printers in 1976–2012." *Journal of Engineering and Technology Management* 42, pp. 31–45.

Hulten, B. 2007. "Customer Segmentation: The Concepts of Trust, Commitment and Relationship." *Journal of Targeting, Measurement and Analysis for Marketing* 15, pp. 256–69.

Kandybin, A. 2009. "Which Innovation Effort Will Pay?" *Sloan Management Review* 51, pp. 53–60.

Lafferty, B.A., and R.E. Goldsmith. 2004. "How Influential Are Corporate Credibility and Endorser Attractiveness When Innovators React to Advertisement for a New High Technology Product?" *Corporate Reputation Review* 7, pp. 24–26.

Lim, C., and T. Fujimoto. 2019. "Frugal Innovation and Design Changes Expanding the Cost-Performance Frontier: A Schumpeterian Approach." *Research Policy* 48, pp. 1016–29.

McLaughlin, P., J. Bessant, and P. Smart. 2008. "Developing an Organization Culture to Facilitate Radical Innovation." *International Journal of Technology Management* 44, pp. 298–323.

Nguyen, T.T., L. Mia, L. Winata, and V.K. Chong. 2017. "Effect of Transformational-Leadership Style and Management Control System on Managerial Performance." *Journal of Business Research* 70, pp. 202–13.

Nguyen, D. 2018. "The Impact of Intellectual Capital and Knowledge Flows on Incremental and Radical Innovation: Empirical Findings from a Transition Economy of Vietnam." *Asia-Pacific Journal of Business Administration* 10, pp. 149–70.

Noel, L., B.K. Sovacool, J. Kester, and G. Rubens. 2019. "Conspicuous Diffusion: Theorizing How Status Drives Innovation in Electric Mobility." *Environmental Innovation and Societal Transitions* 31, pp. 154–69.

Rajagopal 2008. *Globalization Thrust: Driving Nations Competitive.* Hauppauge. New York : Nova Science Publishers.

Rajagopal. 2011. "The Symphony Paradigm: Strategy for Managing Market Competition." *Journal of Transnational Management* 16, pp. 181–99.

Rajagopal. 2016a. *Innovative Business Projects: Breaking Complexities, Building Performance (Vol.2)-Financials, New Insights, and Project Sustainability.* New York, NY: Business Expert Press.

Rajagopal. 2016b. *Sustainable Growth in Global Markets: Strategic Choices and Managerial Implications.* Basingstoke, UK: Palgrave Macmillan.

Rayport, J.F., and B.J. Jaworski. 2004. "Best Face Forward.' *Harvard Business Review* 82, pp. 1–12.

Reeves, M., and M. Deimler. 2011. "Adaptability: The New Competitive Advantage." *Harvard Business Review* 89, pp. 135–41.

Ringberg, T., M. Reihlen, and P. Rydén. 2019. "The Technology-Mindset Interactions: Leading to Incremental, Radical or Revolutionary Innovations." *Industrial Marketing Management* 79, pp. 102–13.

Silva, G.M., C. Styles, and L.F. Lages. 2017. "Breakthrough Innovation in International Business: The Impact of Tech-Innovation and Market-Innovation on Performance." *International Business Review* 26, pp. 391–404.

Sumo, R., W. Valk, A. Weele, and C. Bode. 2016. "Fostering Incremental and Radical Innovation through Performance-Based Contracting in Buyer-Supplier Relationships." *International Journal of Operations & Production Management* 36, pp. 1482–1503.

Ulaga, W., and A. Eggert. 2006. "Value-Based Differentiation in Business Relationships: Gaining and Sustaining Key Supplier Status." *Journal of Marketing* 70, pp. 119–36.

Verganti, R. 2011. "Designing Breakthrough Products." *Harvard Business Review.* 89, no. 10, pp. 114–120.

von Hippel, E., S. Thomke, and M. Sonnack. 1999. Creating Breakthroughs at 3M. *Harvard Business Review* 77, no. 5, pp. 47–57.

Wang, N., Y. Hua, G. Wu, C. Zhao, and Y. Wang. 2019. "Reverse Transfer of Innovation and Subsidiary Power: A Moderated Mediation Model." *Journal of Business Research* 103, pp. 328–37.

Winter, A. and V. Govindarajan. 2015. Engineering Reverse Innovations. *Harvard Business Review* 93, no. 7, pp. 80–89.

Xu, N., and Y. Xu. 2016. "Research on the Key Success Factors of Reverse Innovation of the Latecomer Engineering and Technical Services Enterprises." *Journal of Science and Technology Policy Management* 7, pp. 58–76.

Ye, Q., D. Wang, and W. Guo. 2019. "Inclusive Leadership and Team Innovation: The Role of Team Voice and Performance Pressure." *European Management Journal* 37, pp. 468–80.

Zeschky, M.B., S. Winterhalter, and O. Gassman. 2014. "From Cost to Frugal and Reverse Innovation: Mapping the Field and Implications for Global Competitiveness." *Research Technology Management* 57, pp. 20–17.

Zhou, K.Z., and C.B. Li. 2012. "How Knowledge Affects Radical Innovation: Knowledge Base, Market Knowledge Acquisition, and Internal Knowledge Sharing." *Strategic Management Journal* 33, pp. 1090–1102.

CHAPTER 4

Cognitive Ergonomics

Overview

Ergonomics is concerned with the study of people at work. Cognitive ergonomics focuses on developing knowledge contours and decision constructs in human mind. Consumer behavior is a complex system, and the conditions enhancing knowledge, perceptions, and decision-making abilities broadly constitute cognitive ergonomics. This chapter discusses compatibility between cognitive attributes that are epistemologically explained and the cognitive architecture that is used in socio-economic behavioral processes. The behavioral factors contributed by the intrinsic and extrinsic factors are discussed in this chapter in the context of developing cognitive ergonomics. Consumer perceptions constitute the foundation of cognitive ergonomics. The perceptual mapping, semantics and role of perceived values of consumers are discussed comprehensively in the following text. In addition, this chapter also discusses in brief about the new concept on cognitive anarchy and its implications on consumer behavior.

Behavioral Factors

Frugal innovations, product attractiveness, and the increasing market competition are not the only factors responsible to drive chaos in the market; consumer cognition and volatility in decision making also affect the demand fragmentation, defection, and market entropy. The intrinsic and extrinsic factors drive the judgmental behavior of consumers and construct cognitive ergonomics, which, over time, places consumers in a state of comfort or otherwise. Consumers' judgment, decision making, and behavior depend on the mental processes that determine the consumer consciousness and buying behavior. Indirect measures and associated market developments contribute to a better understanding of conscious and subconscious cognitive processes among consumers that help them in making opted or predetermined consumption judgments. Such cognitive conscience can be explained by understanding the decision perspectives of a consumer intending to buy a can of carbonated drink in a supermarket. As he or she stands in front of the shelf displaying carbonated soda cans, a complex choice grid of various causes and effects is built in his or her mind. Such cognitive matrix affects psychophysical actions and stimulates the decision-making process. The consumer's body signals physiological changes activating his or her senses: touch, sight, smell, and taste that makes him or her take a quick decision (sometimes in confusion) to pick the soda from shelf to his or her cart (Worfel 2019). Therefore, the cognitive ergonomics plays a key role in consumer consciousness and decision making. Accordingly, consumers manage chaos of products and services in the market and determine their cognitive stand with consumption.

Consumers are the conscious agents of change in the marketplace, who are capable of altering the demand for existing products and services by identifying and articulating their needs and desires. Consumer-centric companies, thus, invest heavily in mapping consumer cognition and understanding their implicit preferences to revise product designs and make advertising more appealing to them. Companies based on preference data from surveys, interviews, and focus groups study the consumer behavior (Baumeister et al. 2017). Consumers develop semantic map of values while analyzing a product through the available verbal and nonverbal information and build knowledge base to support the decision process. They systematically estimate the values associated with the products, validate influencing factors, and compare them with the preferences emerged during the subconscious state of mind by analyzing episodic memories. Consumers derive the realm of choices from the merits of the products and congruence of the episodic memories to construct the decision paradigm comprising products offered, knowledge and influence, subconscious cognition, value determinants, and self-actualization. Such paradigms build cognitive ergonomics and explain a wide array of phenomena in decision making.

Intrinsic Factors

Consumer behavior is widely affected by personality-driven factors besides the socio-cultural influences. Of many, there are seven intrinsic factors comprising personality, culture, materialism, shopping tendency, hedonic pleasure, utilitarianism, buying leadership and referrals, and impulsive buying tendency on impulsive buying behavior. Among these, behavioral factors materialism, tendency of lead shopping, arousal and merriment, and impulsive buying behavior exhibit a significant positive relationship with lead buying behavior. In addition, the cultural influence of collectivism combined with extraversion and conscientiousness significantly affect the consumer cognition and buying behavior (Badgayan and Verma 2014). One of the strongest factors influencing consumer behavior is the genetically derived personality, which can be explained as intrinsically learned personality. The behavioral similarities, therefore, grow as an umbrella within a family or community. Personality has unique and dynamic attributes that include physio-psychological determinants to influence cognitive behavior and responses toward decision making. Specific intrinsic behavioral attributes like impulsivity, neuroticism, and extraversion are principally caused by the genetic influences that drive consumption behavior in association with the distinctive personality traits (Bratko et al. 2013).

Most companies are inculcating radical buying behavior among consumers by generating brand literacy through the interactions of consumer communities on social media. Facebook, Twitter, and Instagram have been the principal platforms of consumer networking for most of the consumer-centric companies. Companies explore the consumer needs and preferences on the digital platforms and tend to meet consumers' rising expectations on the products and services they intend to buy. Simultaneously, consumers also stay critical to the multichannel experience of peers on their preferred brands to reaffirm their purchase intentions. Most consumers are unable to make the right buying decision because they do not acquire desired information and analyze the key indicators critically. In an appropriate decision-making exercise, consumers must be able to define their problem carefully and look for an appropriate solution. However, understating the problem and determining *what they want* is a complex question. Consumers make cognitive exercises for getting to the bottom of problem. It largely depends on the level of precision on selecting criteria, determining the scope of available information, and identifying number of substitute options (Sofi and Nika 2017).

Consumer experience is diffused by the user-generated contents on social media, which help them review their perceptions, attitude, and behavior toward a brand in the marketplace. For example, Nordstrom customers can buy products not only in the physical and on the virtual stores, but also through a mobile app, on Instagram, or via text message. Consumers can pick, return, or exchange their online purchases at Nordstrom stores. Such convenience of digital marketing to access reviews and referrals, develop purchase intensions, and the possibility of decision reversals in case of change in the value perceptions has strengthened the consumer attitude and behavior toward the brand. Buying behavior, influenced by extrinsic factors like store ambience, peer reviews, and social status, is an outcome of social and promotional stimuli. Consumers develop their cognitive ergonomics filtering their prime senses and the available product information before shopping. The induced behavior of consumers often emerges as an accidental behavior during the buying process, as it is driven more by the emotional preferences than a predetermined decision. However, the intrinsic elements play significant role and streamline the in-store consumer behavior and decision-making process. Impulsive buying is a spontaneous process that overrides the predetermined consumer cognition. The intrinsic factors affect consumer cognition through an unexpected and unrelenting push for attaining something instantaneously. The desire of buying hedonically complex products often creates emotional conflicts due to asymmetric validation of decision criteria and weak cognitive logic to support intricate decisions. Therefore, impulsive buying often occurs with diminished concerns for its consequences, and responsiveness, and trust toward the brands or products. In other words, consumers tend to develop a strong cognitive base to support any buying decision, which enables them to justify even an impulsive purchase, and compromise with any shortcomings arising because of the spontaneous buy. Emotional elements protect the consumers' feelings, whereas the cognitive elements facilitate self-control or determination in making buying decision (Hoch and Loewenstein 1991).

Most consumers, who are conventionally tuned to decision making, believe in learned experiences and knowledge from predetermined sources like family and community. Consumers often perceive their needs and values incorrectly, which results in distorted or unexpected buying decisions. The behavioral perceptions are biased by analyzing intrinsic effects on buying and consumption decisions because the influence of emotions and perceived risk (individual dimension, intrinsic effects) on the value-oriented decisions affect the decision making of consumers. In addition, derived influence of available information, situational complexity, and extrinsic effects drive consumers to reorient their cognitive ergonomics (Fochmann et al. 2016). The acquired and shared culture among consumers drives awareness about the new trends, which in turn arouses new consumer preferences. The experience sharing over the digital platforms further influences the consumer behavior over a long time. Patterns of consumerism are changing in the society, as there are shifts in the consumer demography in the markets. The explosion of mass consumer segment, urbanization, and increase in the size of the population of aging consumers have contributed significantly to the shifts in consumer preferences and overall consumption behavior. Direct-to-customer marketing strategies, convenience shopping, and social media-driven marketing approaches of companies have increased social and cultural influence on developing the consumer behavior.

Perceptions among consumers is a cognitive process that registers the instant feeling of any product, services, or a situation. It is a process of recognizing sensory stimuli that builds awareness and knowledge base. Consumers develop perceptions by self-generated stimuli and by drawing inferences from other people in the society. The social perceptions make consumers learn about the feelings and emotions from anchor personalities in the society by analyzing information on physical appearance and verbal and nonverbal communication. Self-perception by customers relates to the values and motivations that drive buying behavior. Visual attraction of products, emotions, self-congruence and perceived experience, knowledge and beliefs, and psychosocial insights about the products drive the perceptions of consumers, which helps in developing attitude and behavior in future. Consumers derive their beliefs from the learned culture, self-references, values perceived from the society, and cognitive factors. The effects of ethical beliefs and consumer perceptions on the purchase intention affect the consumer trust. The consumer perceptions are widely derived from consumer involvement in the buying process. Such perceptions on various product-market indicators like attributes, quality, brand, and price help in moderating cognitive relations among consumers, products, channels, and companies. Consumer perceptions are gradually developed as a blend of exploration, enhancement, experience, and emotions. Perceptions do not appear from the blues of product attractiveness, promotions, or visual merchandizing. Therefore, respecting consumer perceptions, ethical beliefs, and social values are important preconditions to understand consumers' needs, demand, and involvement (Banovic et al. 2019).

Consumer perceptions are often agile and need to be endorsed by peers, friends, and family to support decision making and to put them into practice over a long term. Such cognitive process creates consumption attitude among consumers. Perceptions linked to emotions are commonly impulsive and temporary, which do not make a dent on cognitive process continuity, and help in decision making. The perceptions should be measurable. Consumers generally measure their perceived values in reference to the desired satisfaction in terms of value for money derived through the convergence of quality and price. The higher perceived value of consumers not only justifies the quality of perceptual process among the consumers, but also determines the social leadership by way of how many follow a right perception of a consumer as referral. Perceptions of consumers should also be able to analyze the right information at the right time and distinguish the attributes of personal and social determinants that influence the cognitive process.

The consumer philosophy today consists of *touch, feel, and pick* of products and services, wherein the perceptual process among consumers is observed in four stages beginning with sensitive feeling, attention, review, and cognitive affirmation. The consumer perception is backed also by ACCA factors comprising awareness, comprehension, conviction, and action. Advertisements, in-store and online promotions, marketing events, referrals, and social media help in generating awareness among consumers to develop self-perceptions on the products and services. Consumers explore further information on the seeded perceptions to comprehend their knowledge and rationale in developing conviction toward the purchase decisions. Conviction is a state of cognition that builds inclination toward the products or services to buy. Consumer perceptions justified over the conviction may turn into action, as consumers finally buy the products or services (Rajagopal 2011).

Consumer attitudes and behavior are largely governed by the consumer perceptions—learned, acquired, and shared, in emerging and developed markets. The instability in consumer perceptions often lowers the value expectations and inappropriately influences purchase intentions. The theory of impression management lays the conceptual framework incorporating the social (conspicuousness and status), personal (hedonism and materialism), and functional (uniqueness and price-quality perceptions) value perceptions (Shukla 2012). Impression management or the self-presentation approach involves the processes through which people analyze how others perceive them or they perceive others. Consumers are motivated by the companies through promotions, visual merchandizing, and social media to perceive about their brands, values, and associations. Positive perceptions help consumers believe that corporate promotions are relevant to the attainment of desired goals and the goals for which their perceptions are relevant are valuable. However, discrepancy exists between how promotions and campaigns want to be perceived by the consumers and how are they perceived by other. When consumers are motivated to manage their impressions derived from perceptions, they are carried out in social and personal context. The values of the consumers are perceived as self-concepts (Leary 2001).

Internal factors influencing the perceptual process of consumers include propensity of consumer learning on the attributes of products, services, and brands in the market and social ambience. The capability of retaining perceived memories and associated emotions also drives the cognitive process among consumers toward validating their brand perceptions. The perception of consumers toward shopping is commonly influenced by the social-psychodynamics, need, enthusiasm for experimentation, benefit-seeking, and obsessive behavioral attributes. Thus, consumer perceptions influence consumer behavior with their ecosystem, which often creates *me too* feeling, and induces the pro-perception buying decisions. In addition, perceived benefits in terms of

price, associated promotions, and perceived use value of products significantly influence purchase intention. Perceived consumers' effectiveness,
occupation, and income level also have a significant effect on confirming the positive consumer perception toward willingness to pay for the
product of high-perceived value (Zhao et al. 2018).

An attitude among consumers is evolved over the perception, which
is an initial phase of consumer perception on products and services. It
is a stronger dimension of consumer perceptions that embeds a set of
beliefs toward a brand, company, person, product, service, a marketing
or sales event, or a business situation. Attitude can be positive or negative
or can simply appear as a social trend or personal feeling about the product, services, or brands with a strong emotional commitment. Though
attitude formation among consumers is largely influenced by the intrinsic factors, it is also affected by the buying ambience comprising, colors,
lighting, music, display, and in-store information (digital or face-to-face).
For instance, consumers buy more French wine when French music plays
in the store and more German wine when German music plays (North
et al. 1999). Recent evidence from consumer neuroscience supports the
notion of automatic attitude activation by stimulating store ambience
and matching it with the cognitive ergonomics of consumers. This helps
in preference formation among consumers by stimulating neural signals
(Goto et al. 2017).

Self-perception associated with self-congruence among consumers
forms attitude among consumers toward a specific brand. Consumer
attitude is developed based on the self-perception and the opinions they
publicly express on particular issues encouraging social interactions. Consumer attitude is a convergence of perceived expectancy and perceived
value evolved through the cognitive process of consumer perception
(Fishbien and Ajzen 1975). As this convergence turns stronger over time,
it is likely to develop an attitude toward products and services. Consumer-centric companies observe that sustainable attitudes leverage them
toward developing long-term marketing strategies and help them gain
enough time and space for implementing these strategies. A sustainable
attitude among consumers leads to cultivate a behavior in due course of
time. Companies tend to develop consumer attitude through the social
media, brand communication, corporate governance, and customer

value. The buying attitude of consumers toward products stays sustainable, as the perceptions of consumers are governed by the popularity and image through celebrity endorsements and peer expressions in the marketplace. Accordingly, the attitudes of consumers are driven by the social and personal perceptions on product attributes, price, and the perceived use value. The social and celebrity endorsements can significantly influence consumer purchase attitudes via both direct and indirect effects (Sheu 2010).

Consumers develop quick perceptions on the shopping ambience and product attractiveness. These perceptions help in building cognitive ergonomics over time. Shopping center design, management attributes, and public infrastructure in shopping centers constitute the shopping ambience, which affects consumer cognition on buying behavior. Examples of such attributes are the level of maintenance, area for pedestrians, window displays, street layout, and street activities. These external factors support the perceived values and the sense of satisfaction, leading to consumer surplus (Oppewal and Timmermans 1999). Besides, brand anthropomorphism enhances the ability of consumers to recognize the inherent value of brands and strengthen cognitive behavior of consumers toward buying and referrals. Self-image congruence on brands determines brand love, which further enhances consumer value through interpersonal and digital word of mouth. Social networks have a significant influence on the dynamics of consumer cognition and consumption behavior. These networks set a consumption pattern among consumers and develop systems thinking in consumption behavior. A logic framework that helps in orienting cognitive ergonomics among consumers highlights the criticality of the social network (Ruane and Wallace 2013).

Consumer perceptions are sensitive to their experiences and help in building attitude if sustained for a reasonable period. Most consumer-centric companies ensure that consumers gain favorable and sustainable perception through brand campaigns, digital communications, social media forums, and product and services trials. In this perceptual mapping process, the cognitive drivers help consumers in developing sustainable consumer attitude. This situation not only positions the brand as *top-of-mind* element, but also encourages repeat buying among the consumers. Such attitude reflects in the buying behavior and sharing of brand experience extensively over the interpersonal and digital platforms by the consumers. Powerful market stimulants such as advertisements of fashion brands in urban shopping malls have influenced transnational cosmopolitanism and increased the desire for buying among young women consumers. Fashion brands with high level of brand-consumer engagement tend to drive higher value perceptions on *me too* feeling, high self-image congruence, uniqueness, and quality value perceptions of the brand, and such relationships are mediated by credit transactions, which bridge the gap in purchasing power among young women consumers (Ahn et al. 2013).

In order to create positive perceptions among consumers, companies tend to inculcate needs-led perceptions using emotional strategies such as physiological (survival), safety, love, esteem, and self-actualization. In addition, companies learn perceptions and attitudes of consumers, endorsed by the celebrities and over the social media, to strengthen and hold them over the long run. By sharing experience on perceptions and attitude, consumers influence fellow consumers. The experiential marketing helps companies in socializing the brands and gaining competitive advantage in the marketplace. However, perceptions take long time to develop into an attitude. However, building an attitude in the marketplace is often more impulsive than judgmental for consumers, as attitude is largely determined by the pressure of consumer needs, available choices, and sustainable consumer perceptions. Impulsive attitudes emerge out of consumer psychodynamics and peer pressure due to some obsessive attributes of the brands, products, or services, such as low price and sales promotion offers raised by the companies (Rajagopal 2018).

The need for autonomy and differentiation in consumer perceptions, buying attitude, and decision making is explained by the optimal distinctiveness theory, which states that individuals strive to maintain a balance between the need to be assimilated by the peers and family (Sorrentino et al. 2009). The purchase intentions among consumers are affected not only in personal context, but also in the socio-cultural and ethnic values that influence the buying behavior largely. The distinctive features of products broadly include designer brand, celebrity endorsement, and media reviews that are consistently associated with consumer cognition plays the strongest role in determining the buying behavior (Calvo and Marrero 2009). The distinctiveness theory supports the notion that ethnicity can influence consumer responses to various marketing stimuli such as sales promotions and advertisements.

Customer preference and value derived from buying the fashion brands are largely influenced by the differentiation in social personality and self-esteem of the consumers. Consumer experience with high socio-economic power perceptions creates qualitatively distinct psychological motives toward buying fashion brands that develop unique consumption patterns. Love, anthropomorphism, and self-image congruence are the central attributes in the consumer–brand relationship domain among fashion brands (Ismail and Spinelli 2012). Social value and lifestyle, consumer personality, ethnicity, and art are applied as strategic tools in creating fashion brands and influence buying propensity of consumers. It is relevant to achieve an authentic fit to the gender sensitivity and associated brand emotions that helps in developing purchase intentions among consumers. Integrating the discussed brand elements consistently within the whole value chain system leads to a higher brand equity (Jelinek 2018).

The attributes of consumer cognition drive the thinking process of acquired and learned knowledge by way of analyzing perception, reasoning, and judgment, which is guided by rationalism or rational decision-making (Kim et al. 2007). Consumers gain stimuli from brand advertisement, experiential marketing, brand reviews, and product promotions. Such stimuli help consumers in developing emotions and perceptions. Emotions appear as experienced states in the consumer mind, which would ascend out of cognitive appraisal and assessment of circumstances. Emotions generate rational hierarchical effects and guide the cognitive process toward developing perceptions on the circumstantial awareness and knowledge (Yang and Bahli 2015). They influence peoples' beliefs and attitudes, and they help guide their thinking, decision making, and actions. A major attribute of consumer perceptions is the underlying arousal generated during the process of responding to societal and business stimuli in the cognitive process of consumers. In direct-to-customers communication practice, consumers are continuously blitzed with relationship calls and marketing messages, including television commercials, e-mail solicitations, and business circulars of the company. However, persuasion often punches on right customers and stimulates the buying need to elicit the desired response on the prospected product or service. It might be very difficult for a salespeople to identify what drives consumer behavior, largely because there are so many possible combinations of stimuli. Although innovative marketing strategies have always been a creative endeavor toward creating consumer behavior, adopting a scientific approach to it could make the consumer experience process easier and supportive to cognitive perceptions to enhance the customer value (Rajagopal 2016). Various intrinsic factors affecting the cognitive ergonomics are exhibited in Figure 4.1.

Cognitive ergonomics is a science of consumer behavior that is an intangible infrastructure affecting the behavioral organization of consumers and its effects on decision making. Cognition among consumers is grown in five segments comprising intrinsic and extrinsic domains, knowledge management, behavioral sensitivity, and decision making, as illustrated in Figure 4.1. The intrinsic elements that affect the consumer cognition include sensory touchpoints comprising vision, hearing (audition), smell (olfaction), taste (gustation), and touch (somatosensation), leading to generate self-perceptions. The perceptions of self-image congruence and self-referencing develop anthropomorphism among the

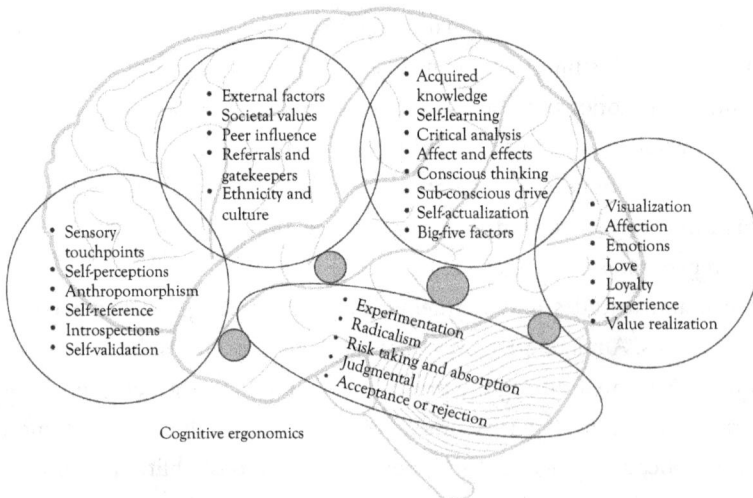

Figure 4.1 Key elements of cognitive ergonomics

Source: Author

consumers, which delivers hedonic pleasure and self-esteem. Often, consumers introspect their personality and match it with the social values to self-validate their choices and build a protected cognitive ergonomics. Most consumer-centric companies in the fashion industry support consumers' mindset to develop such shielded cognitive ergonomics, which helps the companies build prolonged brand loyalty.

The external factors include market dynamics, socio-political developments, and legal frameworks. Consumer cognition is often influenced by the societal values, referrals, and peer reviews within the ethnic and cultural boundaries. Sometimes, with the strong effects of acquired culture and knowledge, consumers tend to choose the values and lifestyles beyond the ethnic and cultural boundaries of the society. Such consumer cognition radicalizes the decision-making process. In addition, acquired knowledge, self-learning, ability to critically analyze the information, and observations based on causes and effects help consumers rationalize their cognitive frameworks. However, cognitive rationales are often disrupted by the subconscious movements and affect conscious thinking. A refined cognitive framework helps consumers reach self-actualization over time. The big five factors comprising extroversion, agreeableness, openness, conscientiousness, and neuroticism are regarded as personality traits, and one or a combination of these factors serve as the foundation of cognitive ergonomics of consumers.

Some other elements that develop behavioral sensitivity consists of visualization, affection, emotions, and love, as exhibited in Figure 4.1. Consumers' association of higher degree with these elements helps them in developing loyalty on products, brands, and services of customer-centric companies. This behavior is further supported by their continuous experience and realization of expected values. Most consumers fail to refine and strengthen their cognitive ergonomics because of their tendency of experimentation, radicalism, risk averseness, and being judgmental on less explored information.

Consumers behave in four different ways in the market—proactive, reactive, interactive, and inactive. All four ways of expressing consumer behavior refer to their cultural background. Proactive consumers are experimental to new products and are prone to accept the cultural changes induced by the market. The proactive consumers are largely induced by the markets through lifestyle interventions and cross-cultural fusion. Reactive consumers are critical to new products, strategies, and corporate initiatives and prefer the conventional culture that has grown over the period in the society. The reactive consumers are aggressive in sharing their experience and are often critical about the products and services of the company. Interactive consumers express their views logically and analyze the products and services of a company rationally and comparatively. Inactive consumers are passive and non-responsive. Consumers in the acquired culture are prone to behavioral changes, adapt to modern values, and are interactive in the market. These attributes of acquired culture drive multinational companies to develop dynamic marketing strategies, build their brand, and augment market share (Rajagopal 2016).

Companies launch customer loyalty programs to motivate consumers to make buying decision for their brands and stay as referrals to other consumers. Companies usually want to retain existing customers, maintain sales levels and profits, increase the potential value of the existing customers, and encourage customers to buy their other products as well by offering continuous motivations to the customers through brand campaigns and social media connections. Motivated consumers not only just buy a brand, but also engage in storytelling about their experience with the loyalty program. Such voluntary contribution to brand promotion helps companies highlight peer motivation and attract new consumers. Therefore, companies develop loyalty programs embedding consumer emotions that serve as motivational driver to deliver a direct or indirect impact in the marketplace. For example, the General Motors rebate scheme builds up savings toward a new car and built perception of value such as more availability of cash with consumers (Dowlings and Uncles 1997).

Brand loyalty is indicative of the consumers' creative mindset, which emerges out of the predetermined cognitive ergonomics. This helps consumers make buying decisions on the basis of awareness, attributes, trial (experience), availability, and propensity for repeat buying. It indicates that there is a commitment to consistently buying and redistributing brand and the associated services in the future, motivating the repeat purchase behavior among consumers. Brand loyalty can be measured in behavioral and attitudinal terms. Behavioral loyalty relates to actual repurchasing behavior, whereas attitudinal loyalty relates to the intention to repurchase, and it affects commitment to a specific product (Kaur et al. 2018). Promotion-focused consumers are motivated by the value for money and visualize their motives to buy the product. They like to be the first to get the offer and avoid stock-out situations. Consumers with promotion-focused buying attitude often exhibit dynamic motivation to the sales offers over the quality and brand reputation. However, quality-focused people see their motives as perceived use value of the product. They are vigilant, risk-averse, thorough, and accurate and like to maintain the status quo. Motivational focus, thus, affects the way consumers want to analyze the motivational information, develop rationale, and make appropriate buying decision. Consumer motivations are all about the way they want to pay attention, frame goals, make decisions, and achieve the consumption goals (Grant and Higgins 2013).

During the cognitive process toward decision making, illustrative cognitive mapping of thoughts helps the consumers and makes sure the prospect absorbs the context and contents of the discussion. The effect of stimulus-response mappings is a difficult process, wherein generating stimuli might differ from the self-reference stimuli acquired by the consumer during his or her search for products or services. Therefore, the degree of consistency and variability of information delivery by the salespeople affect the stimulus-response quality and time of consumers. Cognitive maps track the natural progression of consumers' though process connecting each new thought. Cognitive maps can also be used by the referrals in informal meetings with other consumers, such as a sort of visual agenda on Facebook or live chat in any electronic platform, toward delivering more lively and participatory learning process (Rajagopal 2016).

Extrinsic Factors

External factors such as market economy, culture, social values, vogue, and corporate policies for consumers broadly influence the consumer perceptions, attitude, and consumer behavior. Consumer spending patterns, propensity to consume, pricing and affordability, brand affinity, and product attraction among consumers are determined by the market economic conditions. Prices, interest rates, and credit availability are some of the components of consumer economy with respect to income and wealth that significantly affect the consumer consumption behavior (Barnes and Olivei 2017). Generally, consumers' behavior and preferences toward products and services do not change as a function of economic conditions. Therefore, any adjustments in expenditure patterns during economic contractions or expansions affect the consumption budget. The choice of consumers tend to shift according to the income and expenditure ratio among the consumers (Kamakura and Du 2012). Credit availability and credit interest rates also affect the consumption patterns in the destination countries. It has been observed that an incremental pattern of disposable income and innovation of products in the market is associated with conspicuous consumption. Lower credit interest rate not only increases the consumption level, but also induces greater irresponsibility in credit card use among consumers (Rajagopal 2016).

The economic indicators affecting consumers' buying behavior are the variables used to measure the financial status of families or individuals. The consumption economics is networked along the factors of income, expenditure, products, price, perceived value, satisfaction, and social psychodynamics. The analysis of socio-cultural dimensions is an important consideration in determining the impact of consumer economy and spending behavior. Consumers optimize their buying behavior by analyzing comparative advantages over brands. Convenience of spending using mobile money services has a significant influence on building consumer behavior.

Price indicators are extrinsic factors that affect the consumer preferences, value-for-money perceptions, purchase intentions, consumer experience, and consumer behavior. Most companies attract consumers by offering price discounts. Price promotions not only influence mass consumers, but also drive post-purchase hedonic consumption experience. New experiments of consumer products companies involving real spending and consumption demonstrate that when consumption occurs immediately after payment, emotions in reference to price generate consumption experiences. However, this pattern reverses when the price–value relationship is disrupted and consumption is delayed (Lee and Tsai 2014). Consumers perceptually track the costs and benefits of price offers of the companies for reconciling those costs and benefits on completion of the transaction. Favorable price and promotion strategies for brands develop high-perceived value among consumers, which generates positive psychodynamics to create high demand in the market. The customer value-based approach sets the price of a brand based on the value assigned by the customer, rather than based on costs or on competition.

Lifestyle determinants have proved to be successful in explaining a great deal of influence on the consumption pattern. Ethnicity, knowledge, social customs, peer culture, and self-esteem also motivate consumers to inculcate new perceptions on quality of life and lifestyle, or alter those existing. Consumer culture existing in the society and the language appeal of communications also affect the consumer perceptions, attitudes, and consumption behavior. Material culture affects the level of demand, the quality and types of products demanded, and their functional features, as well as the means of production of these goods and their distribution. The status of gender in society, the family, social classes, group behavior, age groups, and how societies define decency and civility are interpreted differently within every culture. Social institutions are a system of regulatory norms and rules of governing actions in pursuit of immediate ends in terms of their conformity with the ultimate common value system of a community. A word-of-mouth recommendation from a trusted source is perceived to be more influential than corporate communication. Consumers attracted by the product campaigns may feel the taste of traditional marketing. However, word-of-mouth cuts through the traditional advertisements quickly and makes a place in the consumers' mind effectively.

Perceptual Mapping

Consumer perceptions are intangible and affected by the tangible attributes of brands. The tangible elements are associated with color, size, calligraphy, punch line, and reputation of the company, while the consumer cognition is manifested in quality, referrals, and brand relevance. Consumer perceptions on products and brands can be explained as adherence, popularity, ability to maintain price point, portraying social and cultural values, and competitive advantages of the brand. The convergence between the consumer perceptions and brands are continuously negoti-ated and (re-)defined by market players, including manufacturers, dis-tributors, retailers, and consumers, to build consistency in the consumer behavior. At the same time, the consumer perceptions also depend on the brand meaning—verbatim or colloquial. Another research has shown that places and events may also drive the brand experience among various market players (Hetzel 2007).

Perceptions signify expression in a cognitive sense. The perceptions of consumers span across socio-cultural and economic perspectives con-cerning the price, consumer surplus, and macro perspectives of products and services. In addition, consumers also perceive non-price factors such as quality, services, and style toward making a buying decision. Besides the perceptions of consumers of tangible and intangible elements on products and services, a major intervening variable is the online social communities and postings that essentially define or redefine a product or service brand. Previous research studies have acknowledged that the social intervention prompts asymmetrical performance of brands and determines the brand's market power. It has been observed that for-ward integration of manufacturing companies into retailing through the establishment of flagship stores is needed, which provides such com-panies with an opportunity to provide a context for their brand and exercise a level of control over its manifestation (Doyle et al. 2008). Consumer perceptions reveal the brand health of the products. The set of perceptions on brand health elements serve as leading indicators of sales, risk, and potential include brand leadership, attractiveness, dis-tinctiveness, satisfaction, and liabilities. The brand appearance influ-ences brand image, whereas initial brand associations and perceived fit between the new product and the remaining either products (category fit) or the brand image (image fit) can strengthen consumer attitude (Salinas and Perez 2009).

Consumer perceptions tend to identify attributes of the objects that match with the personality and social values. The cognitive state of con-sumers attempts to converge with the personality and social entity. The consumers perceive "familiarity or belongingness with an entity" upon realizing the similarities and dissimilarities between members of the social in-group and various out-groups. This distinction allows the individual to create a social identity. When consumers strongly identify a brand, there is convergence between their self-schema and the entity's schema. It is important to recognize that brand expression is a cognitive measure of the brand personality that develops emotional behavioral and buying inclination of consumers on the brand (Carlson et al. 2009). In the growing competitive markets, most companies tend to drive consumer interactions with the products, services, and brands through tangible (do-it-yourself) and intangible (digital communities) platforms to create top-of-the mind perceptions. Tensile perceptions are usually linked with the episodic memories and stay top of mind, while weak perceptions have relatively less memorability. For example, consumer perceptions of cyber brands demonstrate weak brand identity and often fail to connect the brand with self-image congruence. Extended perceptions gain positive spillover effects from the principle thought (utilitarian or hedonic value) and develop a contextual image that manifests into consumer preference and purchase intentions (Saaksjarvi and Samiee 2011).

Consumers perceive the predetermined objects or information in the conscious and subconscious mind. They later find a tangible support to their perceptions though social and peer discussions. The most important factor in mapping the perceptions is the DNA (diffused neural articulation) of thoughts, which is streamlined from macro- (cloud) to micro (subjective) cognition. In this process, perceptual maps are disrupted by the blind sights, which carry insignificant evidences. Most consumer perceptions are connected to episodic memories and are evolved over time. The major challenge with the consumer perceptions entwined with memories is the degree of effective recall and recognition to support decision making. Sometimes, the perceptions are made unclear due to repetition of thoughts and are dumped, which cannot be retrieved. The perceptions that are evolved over comprehensive information, experience, and emotions might also suffer from the iceberg effect. This effect explains that how consumers after carefully examining the available information, determining perceived values, and supporting their self-image congruence and cognitive maps fail in making impulsive buying-decisions. Consumer perceptions on products, services, or brands evolve through a semantic thought process, which offers variety of options on each perceptual indicator. Figure 4.2 shows the sematic mapping of consumers' perceptions.

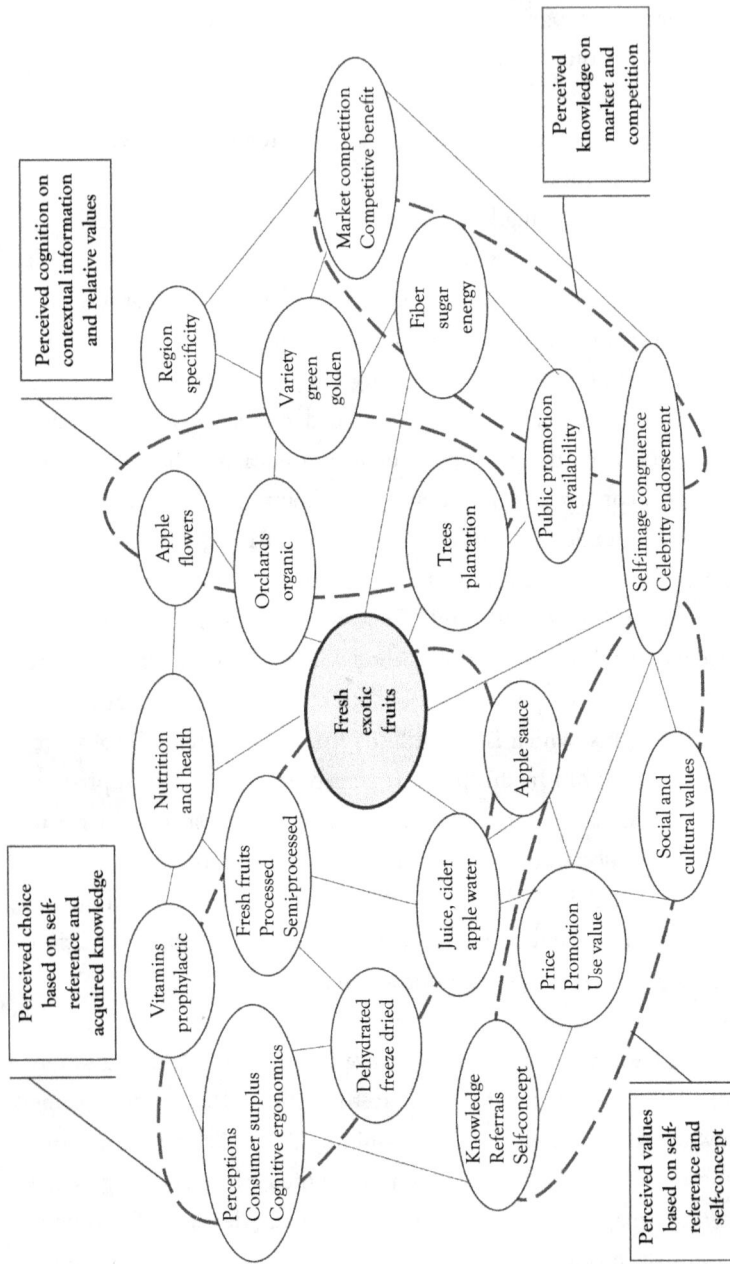

Figure 4.2 Consumer perceptions, semantic mapping, and decision path

Source: Author

Consumers perceive across various contextual propositions on any product or brand and develop cognitive framework to support their decision, as exhibited in Figure 4.2. Consumers map their contextual perceptions in mind prior to deriving values and decisions. Such perceptual maps are called perceptual semantics. The perceptual map of consumers on fresh fruits consumption as an example has been illustrated, which shows that consumers perceive consumption of fresh exotic fruits contextually by analyzing information on product origin, portfolios, and product line. Consumers also analyze the perceived knowledge on markets, competition, and consumer surplus. In addition, the information of referrals and semblance of perceived knowledge is critically analyzed by the consumers for refining the perceptions and deriving perceived value for enabling right decision making. The most complex part of consumer perceptions is to refine the asymmetric choices and derive the ultimate value. In making choices, consumers prioritize self-reference contexts over the referrals, acquired knowledge, product promotions, and corporate image. The perceived values of consumers are refined over time in view of the absolute and derived benefits of products and brands.

Figure 4.3 shows that the cognitive ergonomics defines core areas of perception of a given object or situation, which helps in decision making upon filtering the values. The consumer perception process can be described in six effective stages of perceptions on contextual information, perceptions on acquired knowledge and circumstantial information, perceived values based on self-reference and self-concept, perceptions on choices and self-image congruence, contextual stimuli and perceived decisions, and architecting cognitive ergonomics. These stages of consumer perceptions establish conformity with the perceived decisions over time.

The semantic mapping of perception is a necessary act of cognition among consumers. A consumer standing in front of an aisle of supermarket may be found engaged in perceptual semantics to validate his or her buying decision. The perceptual semantics can be interpreted in the following context:

- Preference
- Connectivity
- Applied significance

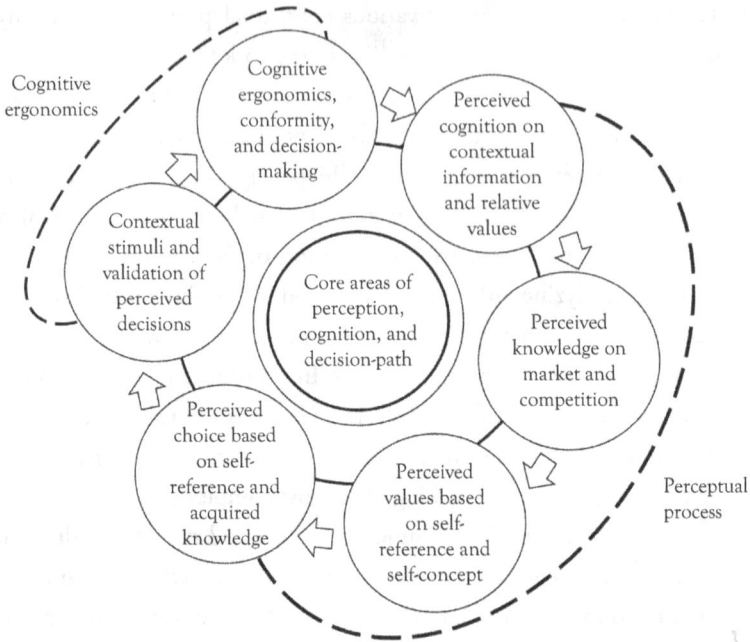

Figure 4.3 Perceptual process, cognitive ergonomics, and decision path

Source: Author

- Conceptual relevance
- Generation of thoughts

Consumer preferences are often complex and can be explained from the utilitarian or hedonic perspectives. The utilitarian preferences often embed the notion of consumer surplus and tend to seek more value out of less paid for. Contrary to this, the hedonic perceptions overrule the value perspectives and honor the emotions of self-actualization and social status. Perceptual semantic maps exhibit linear connectivity on various learning points, which lead to building cognitive ergonomics over time and guide consumers in decision making. Each perceptual value has an applied significance associated with building cognitive ergonomics.

Consumer perceptions largely depend on visual stimuli. There is a significant relationship between visual stimuli and the information, which consumers tend to seek to perceive brands in the market. For example, Asian brands tend to express themselves in the market with reference to perceptions of quality, recognition, consensus in meaning, and *feng shui* (Henderson et al. 2003). It has been observed that learning to see intangible values and symbols as resources is the necessary step in consumer perception. Most companies help consumers to perceive through experience and develop their perceptions based on the brand reality to corroborate their buying decisions. The overall goals and values of consumers are expressed through the perceptions and thus acquire an identity and support them to make an appropriate decision (Urde 1999). There are three kinds of human beliefs, including descriptive, informational, and inferential, that drive the consumer perceptions. Descriptive beliefs derive from direct experience with the objects. Informational beliefs are those influenced by outside sources of information such as ads, friends, and so on. Inferential beliefs are those formed by making inferences (correctly or incorrectly) based on experience, as this experience relates to the current stimuli. Images held in a consumer's mind are one manifestation of these beliefs. Under the effect of communication and previous use, consumers form images about a product's cues that serve as the basis for judgment in future evaluations. Consumer perceptions are reasoned as emotional dynamics in the cognition process toward a specific goal, which consists of functional and symbolic beliefs (Park et al. 1986, Koubaa 2008).

Consumer perceptions guide them to make right choices, leading to the optimal satisfaction from the decision. Individual consumer choices and the social conditions they live in spanning to the economy, society, and environment affect the consumers' decision making. Cognitive models describe the consumer perceptual maps and provide ways to improve their choices with appropriate and refined perceptual interventions. Cognitive science has experimented with large datasets collected in realistic environments on consumer perceptions that play critical role in decision making based on consumer perception of varied nature. Roles of context, representation, and learning in decision making can be better identified by examining consumer choice. The theories of consumption and consumers developed in consumer research represent more than a domain of application as they represent an indispensable part of the behavioral sciences. Conflictive perceptions, or perceptions with insufficient cognitive validity, suffer from similarity syndrome, causing confusion and pushing the decisions in abeyance. Product attraction and compromise effects distract the underlying assumptions and defeat the decision-making process. Most consumer choices engage multiple cognitive functions that govern attention-driven encoding of information, retrieval of right perceptions from memory, eliminating uncertain values, and emphasizing post-choice satisfaction (Bartels and Johnson 2015).

Consumer personality and consumer cognition toward a brand is developed through the social consciousness, community interaction, and etymological emotions. Brand name that has celebrity names, love names, appealing symbols, epical names, historical vigor, and ethno-cultural significance build etymological emotions. The etymological significance helps in developing perceptions, and along with other elements, constructs the cognitive ergonomics of consumers. The theory of etymology explains that symbolic properties of the words and images are associated with the consumer cognition and perception to recognize the products or services. The symbolic meanings are transferred from the verbal and nonverbal communication contents to consumers as they select brands with meanings that are congruent with their self-concept. When the symbolic properties are associated with brands, they are used to construct the self-references or to communicate the self-concept to others. Accordingly, a self-perceived brand connection is formed out of the cognitive abilities of consumers (Smedslund 2011). A consumer may perceive an appropriate symbolic brand meaning derived from etymological evidence and contextually activate self-enhancement goals by confirming the self-perceived brand connections. It is argued in some research studies that humanizing the brands can embed perceptions of consumers within the cognitive ergonomics. Such knowledge can help consumers achieve goals that are motivated by the self-concept connected to the individual preferences. Consumer involvement in brand develops perceptions, possessive behavior, and consumption culture across the temporal dimensions. Possessions can be used to satisfy psychological needs, such as actively creating consumer's self-concept, reinforcing and expressing self-identity, and allowing one to differentiate oneself and assert one's individuality. Possessions can also serve a social purpose by reflecting social ties to family, community, and cultural groups, including brand communities (Escalas and Bettman 2005).

A brand's etymology establishes that non verbalized personality associations of celebrity endorsers on these dimensions can reinforce equivalent consumer beliefs about a brand's fun and stylishness benefits. However, this occurs only if a social consumption context is evoked, and only if the brand image beliefs are appropriate to the consumer schema for the product category involved. Moreover, under these facilitating conditions, such as created brand image beliefs, have an impact only on brand purchase intentions and not on brand attitudes (Batra and Homer 2004). Brand expression of a product or service significantly contributes toward building the brand image and loyalty among consumers. Some interdisciplinary studies reveal that brand identity grows through economic, cultural, sociological, and historical attributes of brand perception among consumers. Brands get involved with the consumers demonstrating product attributes, perceived use value, economic advantage, and image of the company. Brand involvement often triggers product involvement among consumers (Quester and Lim 2003). However, in a competitive marketplace, low brand involvement may be coupled with high product involvement and vice-versa. This is because involvement and loyalty are consumer-defined, not product-defined, phenomena. As a result, it is believed that each involvement and commitment of brand can be thought of as a continuum, along which consumers are distributed (Traylor and Joseph 1984).

Involvement of consumers with products and services builds cognitive associations that help them process and retrieve information on brands and validate them from the utilitarian or hedonic perspectives within the cognitive framework. The positive brand associations create beneficial attitudes and feelings and provide a reason to buy (Aaker 1996). Such brand associations represent the core structure of the memory of consumers over a period. Retrieval from long-term memory occurs when information is recalled through a process of spreading activation. This process involves the activation of one node, which leads to further activation of linked nodes within the mind-map framework of brands in consumers. Some associations are more unique than others. This means that some associations may be shared with many competing brands and may be typical for a product category, while others may be unique to just one or a smaller number of brands (Till et al. 2011, Rajagopal 2016).

Customer-centric value is a set of features that customers like to perceive with the product, services, and corporate image. Consumer perceptions vary in reference to triadic forces of product-brand-company in the marketplace. Often, consumers are not very enlightened to derive a right perception on this triadic power dynamics. A perceived value of consumers may be defined as all of the tangible and intangible assets of key market elements, which a consumer considers necessary to build his or her cognitive ergonomics. Perceived value among consumers increases as the brand becomes better known and as the company supports the brand at different contact points. Therefore, firms tend to continue research and development investment, skillful advertising, and efficient and effective interactions with the trade and with the consumer (Gabay et al. 2009). For instance, to improve the use value of Knorr soups and condiments, Unilever expanded the product line and, at times, advertised the whole line on television by conducting thorough research in India on consumer perceptions and their cognitive ergonomics.

Small firms can compete successfully in the competitive and dynamic markets by developing a strong customer-centric brand value. For example, Palliser Estate Wines of New Zealand is one of the small firms that could manage to develop a strong brand. Adhering to a core set of values, it has ensured the effective use of limited resources and built a competitive advantage through considered action. The Palliser Company, through designing product value, relationship value, entrepreneurial orientation, and market orientation of the brand, has developed the customer-centric value. Integration of these factors led the firm to develop cultural values within the organization, customers, and market players, including suppliers, retailers, bottlers, and so on (Beverland 2004). A key area of controversy on brand manifestation lies in competing approaches to the concept and measurement of brand personality and behavioral loyalty of customers driven by the attitudinal dimensions in getting associated with the brand. Typically, brand loyalty is defined with reference to either attitudinal or behavioral components (Russell-Bennett et al. 2007). Most companies are putting their efforts toward creating pride in the brand by improving the service quality attached to the brand and social networking to build customer loyalty through a sense of derived brand value within consumer community (Bendapudi and Bendapudi 2005).

Cognitive Anarchy

Consumers often face the abnormalities in setting up their preferences, validating their perceptions, and making buying decisions. Failing to correctly map perceptual semantics causes arraying preferences, making appropriate choices, critically examining the self-reference and acquiring information, validating perceived values, and building suitable cognitive ergonomics. Consequently, the consumer decisions are affected adversely and lead to behavioral abnormalities. Cognitive anarchy can be explained as a mental situation that involves high degree of confusion, chaos in handling information, extracting learned and acquired knowledge, and inability to derive rationale perceptions. Such situation causes inconsistency in canvassing preferences with benefits and comparative personal value. The cognitive chaos is also associated with the consumer personality attributes as stated next:

- Extroversion: Adapting to public priorities by overriding self-concepts and innate behavior
- Agreeableness: Submissive to external suggestion and forgoing self-image congruence behavior
- Openness: Adjustability with the community and leading public preferences at the cost of self-reference cognition and perceived values
- Conscientiousness: Changing priorities to please others and adapt to external preferences
- Neuroticism: Low priorities due to moody and experiencing detachable feelings inhibited in anxiety, worry, fear, anger, frustration, envy, jealousy, guilt, depressed mood, and loneliness

In view of these personality traits, consumers are unable to focus on right perceptions to make decisions using self-concepts, self-references, self-image congruence skills, and build comprehensive and consistent cognitive ergonomics. Such cognitive dilemma results into the abnormalities in the buying behavior among consumers leading to minimalism, chaotic buying behavior, unplanned acquisitions, obsessive-compulsive behavior, guilt behavior in buying, and non-viable comparative buying behavior. Cognitive anarchy results into the aforementioned behavioral attributes. Impulse buying behavior often elicits self-conscious emotions, such as guilt and unhappiness, which are quite different from the stress coping strategies. Once guilt is experienced by consumers, avoidant coping strategies are likely to be used, which are associated with less adaptive psychological outcomes (Yi and Baumgartner 2011). Impulsive buying behavior is associated with the coping strategies arising from cognitive chaos, and the intensity of guilt experienced thereof will be positively associated with the cognitive entropy. Cognitive chaos drives fragmentation of goals and associated values. Therefore, consumers behave abnormally on some occasions and are unable to make a rational buying decision. For example, consumers behave abnormally on *Black Friday* as the price discounts and promotions in the stores override the planned buying behavior of consumers, and they run through a cognitive chaos situation. Consumers fail to determine preferences during the cognitive chaos, and the act of shopping mounts over the predetermined goals. In the shopping scenarios today, it has become both a form of entertainment and a rewarding behavior. Consequently, it has become a habit that may be potentially abused by a minority of individuals and leads to a harmful psychiatric problem (Maraz et al. 2015). This phenomenon may be described as compulsive buying behavior emerging out of cognitive chaos.

Summary

This chapter discusses the intrinsic and extrinsic attributes of consumer behavior in the context of consumer perceptions, perceptual mapping, and decision making. Discussions are focused on building appropriate cognitive ergonomics to support decision making. Consumer judgment, decision making, and behavior depend on cognitive processes, which determine the consumer consciousness and buying behavior. Cognitive ergonomics plays a key role in consumer consciousness and decision making. Consumers manage chaos of products and services in the market and determine their cognitive stand with consumption. Consumers develop semantic map of values while analyzing a product through the available verbal and nonverbal information and build knowledge base to support the decision-making process. Of many, there are seven intrinsic factors comprising personality, culture, materialism, shopping tendency, hedonic pleasure, utilitarianism, buying leadership and referrals, and impulsive buying tendency on impulsive buying behavior that affect cognitive ergonomics of consumers. The perceptions of consumers span across socio-cultural and economic perspectives concerning price, consumer surplus, macro perspectives of products and services. Consumers map their contextual perceptions in mind prior to deriving values and decisions. Such perceptual maps are called perceptual semantics. Cognition among consumers is grown in five segments comprising intrinsic and extrinsic domains, knowledge management, behavioral sensitivity, and decision making. External factors such as market economy, culture, social values, vogue, and corporate policies for consumers broadly influence the consumer perceptions, attitude, and consumer behavior.

Buying behavior influenced by the extrinsic factors like store ambience, peer reviews, and social status is an outcome of social and promotional stimuli. Consumers develop their cognitive ergonomics, filtering their prime senses and the available product information before engaging in shopping. Patterns of consumerism are changing in the society, as there are shifts in the consumer demography in the markets. Consumers develop perceptions by self-generated stimuli and by drawing inferences from other people in the society. Consumers derive their beliefs from the learned culture, self-references, and values perceived from the society and cognitive factors. Consumer perceptions are often agile and need to be endorsed by peers, friends, and family to support decision making and to put them into practice over a long term. Positive perceptions help consumers believe that corporate promotions are relevant to the attainment of desired goals, the goals for which their impressions are relevant and valuable, and a discrepancy exists between how they want to be perceived and how other people perceive them. A sustainable attitude among consumers leads to cultivating a behavior in due course of time. The experiential marketing helps companies socialize brands and gain competitive advantage in the marketplace. However, perceptions take a long time to develop into an attitude. The chaos of information and inability of consumers in developing right perceptual semantics cause cognitive inconsistency in decision making. Cognitive anarchy can be explained as a mental situation that involves high degree of confusion, chaos in handling information, extracting learned and acquired knowledge, and inability to derive rationale perceptions.

References

Aaker, D.A. 1996. *Building Strong Brands*. New York, NY: Free Press.

Ahn, T., Y. Ekinci, and G. Li. 2013. "Self-Congruence, Functional Congruence, and Destination Choice." *Journal of Business Research* 66, pp. 719–23.

Badgaiyan, A.J., and A. Verma. 2014. "Intrinsic Factors Affecting Impulsive Buying Behavior-Evidence from India." *Journal of Retailing and Consumer Services* 21, pp. 537–49.

Banovic, M., M.J. Reinders, A. Claret, L. Guerrero, and A. Krystallis. 2019. "One Fish, Two Fish, Red Fish, Blue Fish: How Ethical Beliefs Influence Consumer Perceptions of 'Blue' Aquaculture Products?" *Food Quality and Preference* 77, pp. 147–58.

Bartels, D.M., and E.J. Johnson. 2015. "Connecting Cognition and Consumer Choice." *Cognition* 135, pp. 47–51.

Batra, R., and P.M. Homer. 2004. "The Situational Impact of Brand Image Beliefs." *Journal of Consumer Psychology* 14, pp. 318–30.

Baumeister, R.F., C.J. Clark, J. Kim, and S Lau. 2017. "Consumers (and Consumer Researchers) Need Conscious Thinking in Addition to Unconscious Processes: A Call for Integrative Models, a Commentary on Williams and Poehlman." *Journal of Consumer Research* 44, pp. 252–57.

Bendapudi, N., and V. Bendapudi. 2005. "Creating a Living Brand." *Harvard Business Review* 87, pp. 124–33.

Beverland, M. 2004. "Brand Value, Convictions, Flexibility and New Zealand Wine." *Business Horizons* 47, pp. 53–61.

Bratko, D., A. Butkovic, and M. Bosnjak. 2013. "Twin Study of Impulsive Buying and Its Overlap with Personality." *Journal of Individual Differences* 34, pp. 8–16.

Calvo, M.G., and H. Marrero. 2009. "Visual Search of Emotional Faces: The Role of Affective Content and Featural Distinctiveness." *Cognition & Emotion* 23, pp. 782–806.

Carlson, B.D., D.T. Donavan, and K.J. Cumiskey. 2009. "Consumer-Brand Relationships in Sport: Brand Personality and Identification." *International Journal of Retail & Distribution Management* 37, pp. 370–84.

Doyle, S.A., C.M. Moore, A.M. Doherty, and M. Hamilton. 2008. "Brand Context and Control: The Role of the Flagship Store in B&B Italia." *International Journal of Retail & Distribution Management* 36, pp. 551–63.

Escalas, J.E., and J.R. Bettman. 2005. "Self-Construal, Reference Groups, and Brand Meaning." *Journal of Consumer Research* 32, pp. 378–89.

Fishbien, M., and I. Ajzen. 1975. *Belief, Attitude, Intention, and Behavior: An Introduction to Theory and Research.* Reading, MA: Addison-Wesley.

Fochmann, M., K. Hemmerich, and D. Kiesewetter. 2016. "Intrinsic and Extrinsic Effects on Behavioral Tax Biases in Risky Investment Decisions." *Journal of Economic Psychology* 56, pp. 218–31.

Gabay, G., H.R. Moskowitz, J. Beckley, and H. Ashman. 2009. "Consumer Centered 'Brand Value' of Foods: Drivers and Segmentation." *Journal of Product & Brand Management* 18, pp. 4–16.

Goto, N., F. Mushtaq, D. Shee, X.L. Lim, M. Mortazavi, M. Watabe, and A. Schaefer. 2017. "Neural Signals of Selective Attention Are Modulated by Subjective Preferences and Buying Decisions in a Virtual Shopping Task." *Biology and Psychology* 128, pp. 11–20.

Hoch, S.J., and G.F. Loewenstein. 1991. "Time-Inconsistent Preferences and Consumer Self-Control." *Journal of Consumer Research* 17, pp. 492–507.

Henderson, P.W., J.A. Cote, S.M. Leong, and B. Schmitt. 2003. "Building Strong Brands in Asia: Selecting the Visual Components of Image to Maximize Brand Strength." *International Journal of Research in Marketing* 20, pp. 297–313.

Hetzel, P. 2007. "Fashion as the Ultimate Experiential Object." In A. Carù and B. Cova (eds.) *Consuming Experience* (pp. 126–136). New York: Routledge.

Ismail, A.R., and G. Spinelli. 2012. "Effects of Brand Love, Personality and Image on Word of Mouth: The Case of Fashion Brands among Young Consumers." *Journal of Fashion Marketing and Management: An International Journal* 16, pp. 386–98.

Jelinek, J.S. 2018. "Art as Strategic Branding Tool for Luxury Fashion Brands." *Journal of Product & Brand Management* 27, pp. 294–307.

Kaur, D., M.D. Mustika, and B Sjabadhyni. 2018. "Affect or Cognition: Which Is More Influencing Older Adult Consumers' Loyalty?" *Heliyon* 4, pp. 1–15.

Kim, H.W., H.C. Chan, and Y.P Chan. 2007. "A Balanced Thinking-Feeling Model of Information Systems Continuance." *International Journal of Human-Computer Studies* 65, pp. 511–25.

Koubaa, Y. 2008. "Country of Origin, Brand Image Perception, and Brand Image Structure." *Asia Pacific Journal of Marketing and Logistics* 20, pp. 139–55.

Leary, M.R. 2001. "Psychology of Impression Management." In eds. N.J. Smelser and P.B. Baltes, *International Encyclopedia of the Social & Behavioral Sciences, Pergamon,* 7245–48.

Lee, L., and C.I. Tsai. 2014. "How Price Promotions Influence Postpurchase Consumption Experience Over Time." *Journal of Consumer Research* 40(5), pp. 943–959.

Maraz, A., A. Eisinger, B. Hende, R. Urbán, B. Paksi, B. Kun, G. Kökönyei, M.D. Griffiths, and Z. Demetrovics. 2015. "Measuring Compulsive Buying Behaviour: Psychometric Validity of Three Different Scales and Prevalence in the General Population and in Shopping Centres." *Psychiatry Research* 225, pp. 326–34.

North, A.C., D.J. Hargreaves, and J. McKendrick. 1999. "The Influence of In-Store Music on Wine Selections." *Journal of Applied Psychology* 84, pp. 271–76.

Oppewal, H., and H. Timmermans. 1999. "Modeling Consumer Perception of Public Space in Shopping Centers." *Environment and Behavior* 31, pp. 45–65.

Park, C.W., J.B. Jaworski, and J.D. MacInnis. 1986. "Strategic Brand Concept-Image Management." *Journal of Marketing* 50, pp. 35–45.

Quester, P., and A.L. Lim. 2003. "Product Involvement/Brand Loyalty: Is There a Link?" *Journal of Product & Brand Management* 12, pp. 22–38.

Rajagopal. 2011. "Impact of Radio Advertisements on Buying Behaviour of Urban Commuters." *International Journal of Retail and Distribution Management* 39, pp. 480–503.

Rajagopal. 2016. *Sustainable Growth in Global Markets: Strategic Choices and Managerial Implications*. Basingstoke, UK: Palgrave Macmillan.

Rajagopal. 2018. *Consumer Behavior Theories: Convergence of Divergent Perspectives with Applications to Marketing and Management*. New York, NY: Business Expert Press.

Ruane, L., and E. Wallace. 2013. "Generation Y Females Online: Insights from Brand Narratives." *Qualitative Market Research: An International Journal* 16, pp. 315–35.

Russell-Bennett, R., J.R. McColl-Kenned, and L.V. Coote. 2007. "Investment, Satisfaction and Brand Loyalty in a Small Business Service Setting." *Journal of Business Research* 60, pp. 1253–60.

Saaksjarvi, M., and S. Samiee. 2011. "Relationships among Brand Identity, Brand Image and Brand Preference: Differences between Cyber and Extension Retail Brands over Time." *Journal of Interactive Marketing* 25, pp. 169–77.

Salinas, E.M., and J.M.P. Perez. 2009. "Modeling the Brand Extensions' Influence on Brand Image." *Journal of Business Research* 62, pp. 50–60.

Sheu, J.B. 2010. "A Hybrid Dynamic Forecast Model for Analyzing Celebrity Endorsement Effects on Consumer Attitudes." *Mathematical and Computer Modelling* 52, pp. 1554–69.

Shukla, P. 2012. "The Influence of Value Perceptions on Luxury Purchase Intentions in Developed and Emerging Markets." *International Marketing Review* 29, pp. 574–96.

Smedslund, J. 2011. "Meaning of Words and the Use of Axiomatics in Psychological Theory." *Journal of Theoretical & Philosophical Psychology* 31, pp. 126–35.

Sofi, S.A., and F.A. Nika. 2017. "Role of Intrinsic Factors in Impulsive Buying Decision: An Empirical Study of Young Consumers." *Arab Economic and Business Journal* 12, pp. 29–43.

Sorrentino, R.M., C. Seligman, and M.E. Battista. 2007. "Optimal Distinctiveness, Values, and Uncertainty Orientation: Individual Differences on Perceptions of Self and Group Identity." *Self and Identity* 6, pp. 322–39.

Till, B.D., D. Baack, and B. Waterman. 2011. "Strategic Brand Association Maps: Developing Brand Insight." *Journal of Product & Brand Management* 20, pp. 92–100.

Traylor, M.B., and W.B. Joseph. 1984. "Measuring Consumer Involvement in Products: Developing a General Scale." *Psychology and Marketing* 1, pp. 65–77.

Urde, M. 1999. "Brand Orientation: A Mindset for Building Brands into Strategic Resources." *Journal of Marketing Management* 15, pp. 117–33.

Worfel, P. 2019. "Unravelling the Intellectual Discourse of Implicit Consumer Cognition: A Bibliometric Review." *Journal of Retailing and Consumer Services, Art* 101960. https://doi.org/10.1016/j.jretconser.2019.101960.

Yang, I., and B. Bahli. 2015. "Interplay of Cognition and Emotion in IS Usage: Emotion as Mediator between Cognition and IS Usage." *Journal of Enterprise Information Management* 28, pp. 363–76.

Yi, S., and H. Baumgartner. 2011. "Coping with Guilt and Shame in the Impulse Buying Context." *Journal of Economic Psychology* 32, pp. 458–67.

Zhao, R., Y. Geng, Y. Liu, X. Tao, and B. Xue. 2018. "Consumers' Perception, Purchase Intention, and Willingness to Pay for Carbon-Labeled Products: A Case Study of Chengdu in China." *Journal of Cleaner Production* 171, pp. 1664–71.

CHAPTER 5

Managing Market Chaos

Overview

Chaos in the market is often an unwarranted phenomenon. However, it can be predicted with the help of heuristics and business analytics under some predefined assumptions. Most companies face critical challenges in managing chaos in the market and achieve goals by determining an optimal path. Thus, embracing chaos seems to be an asymmetric approach and risk-averse planning. This chapter draws managerial implications to control market chaos and manage business under uncertainty in the context of competitive market dynamics, market entropy, innovation and technology, and cognitive ergonomics affecting consumer perceptions and strategic marketing decisions of the company.

It is not always the marketing competition to be blamed for creating chaos in the market. There are many elements from frugal innovations to consumers, and niche market players to multinational companies that contribute to the chaos in the market. Consumers portray two dominating instincts: quick solutions and value for money. While exhibiting these concerns, consumers of the mass geo-demographic segment also expect to reach out the products and services at low price with high consumer surplus. In the early 20th century, companies did not have many options to meet such combinations to cater to consumer preference. But, with the continuous growth of innovation and technology applications, frugal innovations in niche markets can serve as cost-effective solutions to consumers, enhancing the perceived value for money. This has been a good beginning in some markets, but competitors replicate frugal innovation in lateral and large markets to attract customers using commercial brands. Manifold growth of frugal innovation products in macro-markets causes chaos and disruption in the markets. In addition, large companies identify successful innovations in the niche markets and acquire them for mass-production to serve mass-markets. Such business drives allow companies to invest in commercializing reverse innovations and to move to the bottom of the pyramid of the market, where such innovations are nurtured at small enterprises. Small enterprises want to grow global, while large companies move down to cannibalize the market share of small enterprises at the bottom of the pyramid. Such bidirectional dynamics in business leads to Darwinism that explains evolution.

Competitive Market Dynamics

In the context of business, Darwinian principles of *struggle for existence* and *survival of the fittest reveal* that the phenomenon of continuous evolution of firms within vertical and horizontal market competition drive the business dynamics. Expanded product-mix across the product portfolios and increase in the length of product line drive the vertical expansion. This occurs within the product portfolios of a predetermined market. Contrary to this, horizontal expansion of business is found across the geo-demographic segments and destinations. Such strategic swings of companies in business cause 3Cs comprising chaos, crisis, and complexity within industry and affect the behavior of consumers. In the past, several studies explained the attributes of market chaos. A competitive market could be chaotic and may operate as a cobweb model with convergence of multiple factors, leading to asymmetric structure and marginal probability of profit (Waters 2009). The theory of chaos in economics has brought valuable insights about how economic systems behave and help people to understand the economic phenomena. Innovation and technology play as stimulants to business growth and drive firms to get competitive advantage in the market. The growth of frugal innovations led by technological advancements brings down the production cost, augments the production efficiency, and delivers better product quality to firms. Accordingly, firms pay more attention to technological innovation despite the threat of market chaos (Li and Wang 2019). Such situation is evident in the oligopolistic markets today led by China, India, and Brazil.

Chaos in market exhibits a nonlinear and fuzzy behavior, which is largely unpredictable. Though, there are exceptional situations that increase the probability of predicting chaotic market consequences for a while. However, chaos has random effects, driving consumers in a dilemma to respond to the uncertain marketing strategies of the companies. Therefore, to focus on gaining consumer surplus in chaotic markets, consumers make buying decisions based on social preferences. It is because peers have the power to shape consumer perceptions and consumption behavior. Such peer effects resulting from social interactions are identified in the context of financial investment, health and diet products, and fashion products (Jungeilges and Ryazanova 2019). Companies developing consumer products for the mass-market segment can experiment differentiation strategy in product-mix and position products taxonomically in the markets that demonstrate consumer demand for the differentiated products. This strategy exhibits colonizing the products and developing specialized niches for consumers to overcome the chaotic effects of markets.

As large companies tend to sponsor frugal and reverse innovations to open marketing avenues in the mass-market and bottom-of-the-pyramid segments, they adhere to an emerging philosophy of *welfare marketing*. This corporate philosophy envisages that every consumer, irrespective of economic and geographic discrimination, has the right to buy global brands. Such strategy has increasingly attracted the business concerns of companies to build niche markets with frugal innovations that are specific to region, social behavior, and ethnicity. Consequently, the growing corporate niches in business-to-consumer and business-to-business market segments have emerged as the right business strategy to avoid market chaos and nurture the brands. Niche markets are ambidextrous and serve either exclusive premium or mass-markets consumers. For example, Elektra (a Salinas Group Company, Mexico) brand in Mexico and Latin America serve the consumers of low-income profile, who are categorically located in the bottom of the pyramid. The large departmental store Macy's serve the consumers who spread geo-demographically across the mass-market segment in the United States. Contrary to this, Harrods and Burberry in the United Kingdom focus on the premium consumer segments whose purchasing power is relatively higher than other consumer segments. These retailing companies are not affected by market chaos, as they have cordoned their markets and consumers.

There are two main challenges in achieving the desired profitably at niche markets, which include shifts in the consumers' behavior and changing the product manufacturing (principal and complimentary attributes of products) and operations (product delivery and services) practices. To ensure success in business, companies need to develop an opportunity map along a spectrum from the least complex and resource-intensive to the most complex factors. Accordingly, companies work on developing market-specific strategies. Companies can develop strategies to explore categorical marketing opportunities in emerging, growing, and mature markets. There exists the opportunities for growth markets that need efforts to redesign products, extend distribution channels, or create new ones. The emerging start-up enterprises at the niche markets continuously venture to develop new products through frugal innovations and aim at triggering price competition outside the niche as their success is voiced by the consumers and stakeholders. The open niches expand into *greenfield markets* and help the companies develop new business models and co-create new markets with the large companies operating in a regional, national, or global marketplace (Simanis and Duke 2014).

Chaos in business drives cannibalization behavior of companies in the market. Various competing products and services, which conform to both principles of Darwinism—survival of the fittest and struggle for existence—are susceptible to price wars, promotion (consumer benefits), pace (first-mover advantage), people (sales and customer relations), and psychodynamics (power of consumer communities). Therefore, cannibalization is considered as an effect of market chaos caused due to high competition among identical and similar products. Cannibalization in the global marketplace is very common in the liberal entry policies adopted by many countries in response to globalization. It has also become a critical phenomenon in selling products and services of identical nature in the competitive consumer segment.

In the growing competitive markets, large and reputed firms are developing strategies to construct innovative combinations of products and services as *high-value integrated solutions* tailored to each customer's needs than simply *moving downstream* into services. Such firms are developing innovative combinations of service capabilities such as operations, business consultancy, and finance required to provide complete solutions to each customer's needs in order to augment the customer value toward the innovative or new products. It has been argued that the integrated solutions are attracting firms, traditionally based in manufacturing and services to occupy a new base in the value stream centered on *systems integration* using internal or external sources of product designing, supply, and customer-focused promotion (Rajagopal and Rajagopal 2007).

Oligopolistic markets are akin to the free markets today, which trigger chaos both at the high- and low-end markets. These markets closely analyze consumer touchpoints and focus on the marketing-mix elements that are sensitive to consumers. Customer-centric companies in oligopolistic market can protect their stakeholder value, increase market share, reduce the incidence of customer defection, and minimize the probability of market fragmentation by adapting to the following strategy in their marketing-mix:

- Product (attributes mapping, complementarity of products, and product lifecycle)
- Price (competitive pricing)
- Place (360-degree availability, convenience, faster and secured deliveries)
- Promotion (hands-on and future benefits and value additions)
- Packaging (attractive, stackable, and cost-effective)
- People (high standards of customer relations, responsiveness, and sensitive to clients)
- Performance (co-creating consumer surplus, reinforcing values, and lessons drawn from product line performance)
- Psychodynamics (creating consumer communities, encouraging digital interface, experience sharing, triggering grapevine effect, crowdsourcing ideas, and managing diffusion of values)
- Posture (reinforcing corporate image, encouraging consumer engagement, co-designing products and strategies, developing differentiated niches to cater to consumer values by the geo-demographic attributes)
- Proliferation (customer-centric product diversification, introducing servitization policies, planning value-based market expansion, and developing competitive differentiation)

The preceding marketing-mix strategies would help companies to sustain oligopolistic competition and manage the threats of market entropy. Staying prepared by taking customers into confidence is one of the effective ways to combat with market chaos caused due to price competitiveness, low-end competing products of new entrants, substitution effect, and demand fragmentation due to bargaining of consumers and suppliers. Companies need to systematically learn competitors' signals and strategies to understand market complexity caused due to the various attributes of competition. Organizational learning is also a cognitive process understanding of array the information, infusing data with right interpretations, and drawing inferences. Commonly, competition information needs to be fragmented and analyzed to learn about competitors' strategy.

Controlling Market Entropy

Market entropy broadly refers to fragmentation of markets from larger operations size to niche markets. The advancement of innovation and technology along the growth in market competition has driven the conventional markets to fragment in small niches across specialized products and services and geo-demographic segments. Large markets are breaking into smaller segments because of shifts in consumer preferences, increasing similar product options, low market effectiveness, low market activeness, and high price volatility. Moreover, due to the difference in the desired transaction volume and market uncertainty in gaining predetermined market share, there are obvious differences in managing the markets at the growth stage. Such business conditions cause market entropy and drive the companies to shift the narrower market space (Liu et al. 2019).

Companies with their specialized product portfolios aim at delivering higher values to customers and create corporate and brand loyalty than competing with new entrants in a less unfamiliar competitive marketplace. Therefore, companies that adapt to such business philosophy choose to operate in the niche market. It allows to develop consistency in market share, profitability, and business growth. However, companies should be able to manage the radical changes in consumer preferences over time, which stimulate changes in consumption patterns. Such changes fragment markets with pre-established demand in the long run. In order to protect markets from such demand disruption and fragmentation of demand, companies can focus on developing customer loyalty strategies and reorient their buying attitude. Good companies invest in building a pool of effective referrals and gatekeepers to acquire new customers and retain the existing customers. Such strategy can help in protecting any structural damage to the market built over time and ensure stability in the market ecosystem.

As the contemporary market ecosystem encompasses high inflow of frugal innovations, dynamic pricing sensitizes changes in the consumer behavior through digital interaction of consumers. An enhanced outreach to consumer communities can be management by the companies with enhanced scope of information. However, the inflow of information in the digital channels is largely unstructured, which drives amateur decisions among consumers raising the possibilities of brand defections and demand fragmentation across the marketplaces. Consumer-centric companies are susceptible to simulated chaos in the marketplace due to frequent disruptions in preferences and demands, causing market entropy. Successful consumer-centric companies are aggressively implementing hybrid business cultures in their organization. Evolution of niche companies with the companies across the geo-demographic segments (domestic delivery services and digital dinning and leisure platforms) is a phenomenon that often reflects deep structural changes in the progressive business models. Business-to-consumer and business-to-business companies need to implement structural reforms to differentiate their strategy and protect fragmentation of their markets by strengthening consumer products markets, financial markets, digital markets, creating community platforms, and commercializing affordable innovation and technology. Therefore, market restructuring appears to be a major challenge to meet the changing business scenarios within the industry and market.

There are three streams of strategic thoughts that can be critically examined by companies to restructure strategies and redesign business models to reduce the influence of cyclical asymmetric behavior of market governing factors. Among these factors, demand cyclicality, fragmentation of markets, market chaos, and customer defections largely affect the market entropy. In order to follow the business restructuring process, companies need to evaluate the existing adaptive marketing capabilities, improve dynamic capabilities, and redesign business models based on resource-advantage (R-A) convergence. In the dynamic, hypercompetitive global economy today, strategies must be focused on companies' abilities to constantly renew themselves in the marketplace (Hunt and Madhavaram 2019). These three streams have implications to manage outside-in or inside-out business situations of companies. Such strategic thrust of companies can help them to stay dynamic against the radical business scenarios like market entropy.

Innovation and Technology

Frugal innovations have become the principal products for success in the low-end markets (mass and lower mass-market segment). Successful companies focus on *design-to-market* strategies to promote mass market innovation products and acquire new consumers within the niche market segments. Managing an innovation value chain consistently through co-creating commercial innovation ideas, converting them to demand objects, and diffusing them among the customers and market players are the major challenges for the innovation companies. Using the innovation stage-gate framework, managers get an end-to-end view of their innovation efforts. Frugal innovations are often considered as low-end market disruptors in emerging markets. However, there exists an uphill task for emerging companies to strengthen the brand equity of innovation and technology-led products and overcome the disruptive innovations.

Innovation lifecycle moves through the common lifecycle comprising introduction, growth, maturity, and decline in the context of market behavior. Firms need to foster the strategies of 4As to strengthen the product awareness, acceptance, availability, and affordability in order to reduce the market risk and gain competitive advantage of the new product in the marketplace. Innovation companies should develop advisory functional teams involving employees, market players, stakeholders, and sponsoring authorities to implement 4As. These functional teams should be empowered to explore competitive differentiation and market leadership prospects, acquire consumers, and develop new buying preferences.

AN emerging business organization can be benefitted by developing a continuous learning process with clear strategy, rightly placed and measured decision metrics, and management models. The business models supported by the stage-gate paradigm would help in managing incremental innovations and co-create a working platform for all market players. Developing contemporary marketing capabilities and competencies can help the enterprises to attain higher spatial and temporal performance. Companies engaged in marketing new products based on frugal innovation should explore opportunities by creating high consumer awareness about the cost effectiveness and utilitarian values of the products and services. Such strategy would help companies to gain myopic advantages in larger markets against the competitors (Atherton 2007). In addition, the servitization concept as a new tool supports integrated growth of organization encompassing manufacturing, technology, and services marketing for developing market penetration strategies in a competitive marketplace.

Vertical or incremental innovations are affected adversely if the brand name or extension differs from the previous brand, as consumers are often unable to relate with their experiences of the previous brand and rebuild trust with the incremental version of the product. Reverse innovation is commercially regarded by many large companies across destinations to promote low-cost products in the global markets. Reverse innovation plays an important role in developing low-cost and utilitarian products for commercialization in the global markets. Commercializing reverse innovation is a disruptive leap to hit a product in the target market, and it demands to develop organizational insight into how a new product could drive an impact in an emerging market. Consumer surplus is one of the major criterion for marketing frugal innovation products. Most customer-centric companies focus on delivering consumer value by promoting consumer psychodynamics. Companies also need to analyze various cognitive dimensions like *me too* feeling, brand loyalty, referral impacts, and brand–consumer defection. In addition, variables affecting sensory marketing, social psychology, and anthropomorphic effect of innovations should also be examined in developing appropriate business models to safeguard against the adversities of the market entropy.

Reverse innovation is the principal source to co-create and promote low-cost utilitarian products for commercialization in the global markets.

Commercializing reverse innovation is a leap of dynamic strategies built around consumer preferences and value-led demand to hit a product in the target markets. The fundamental driver of reverse innovation consists of disposable income of consumers, consumer culture, cost of innovation, and the price of deliverable to the end users. Multinational companies are increasingly showing interest in collaborating with the local companies to acquire and commercialize reverse innovation products with the design-to-market strategies for consumers in low-income market segments across countries, and then adapt the products to the markets of developed economics as disruptive offerings. Despite the growing attractiveness of reverse innovations, adapting to the innovative ecosystem of local companies is not an easy task for large companies that operate on business models governed by the systems thinking. Accordingly, these companies operate through time-tested methods, struggle to overcome the constraints, and leverage the customized short lifecycle of innovations managed by the local companies. Local companies experience common entrepreneurial gaps that prevent them from commercializing innovations by matching segments to existing products, lowering price by introducing selective features, unmask all technical requirements, managing stakeholders' value, and creating global appeal for local products. Large companies collaborating with local companies to manage niche-based innovations in global markets need to strengthen utilitarian values and develop strategies to deliver higher consumer surplus with extended lifecycle of innovative products, such as a low-cost and low-efforts wheelchair for rough terrains. Value-added attributes of reverse innovation help commercialization of innovations faster against the competing products (Winter and Govindarajan 2015).

Companies engaged in bringing up the breakthrough innovations continuously face the challenge of exploring the right consumer preferences. Breakthrough innovations are also susceptible to market entropy during the lifecycle. Market innovations are grown on the product concept that offer high customer surplus and utilitarian values over the conventional products. The diffusion and adaptation of innovations have social, economic, and personal challenges among consumers. In order to make innovations of niche markets successful in large markets, large companies tend to manage radical change from below (local market) combined with judicious leadership from above (corporate behavior). Small innovation teams set audacious goals, improve organizational culture, and adopt to new design methods (Govindarajan 2012).

Managing Cognitive Ergonomics

Innovations often fail, as innovators are unable to analyze consumer behavior, and simultaneously, consumers are also unable to express rationally their needs, beliefs, and perceived values. Fundamentally, consumers are emotional and work with cognitive ergonomics, which allows systematically plotting perceptual maps under different buying situations. Such cognitive dimensions influence the decision-making abilities of consumers over time embedding several common biases. Therefore, companies intending to achieve market leadership need not only to develop market competitiveness, but also to be able to analyze consumer behavior toward innovations and their adaptability (Soman 2014). Consumer judgment, decision making, and behavior depend on cognitive processes, which determines the consumer consciousness and buying behavior. As cognitive ergonomics play a key role in consumer consciousness and decision making, it is necessary for the companies to evaluate the changes in perceptual maps periodically to understand the growing differences in the preferences, demand, customer touchpoints, and value-based beliefs on products. Accordingly, companies restructure their marketing strategies to brand the innovations and reposition them to exploit large market territories. Companies have long used perceptual mapping to understand how consumers feel about their brands relative to competitors', to find gaps in the marketplace, and to develop appropriate customer-marketing strategies. Innovations are sensitive business propositions, and analysis of perceptual maps of consumers helps companies to make appropriate decisions on their marketing and sales. In addition, planning for market share, growth rate, and profitability can be based on the indications of cognitive perceptions of consumers (Dawar and Bagga 2015).

Cognition among consumers is grown in five segments comprising intrinsic and extrinsic domains, knowledge management, behavioral sensitivity, and decision making. External factors such as market economy, culture, social values, vogue, and corporate policies for consumers broadly influence the consumer perceptions, attitude, and consumer behavior. The intrinsic and extrinsic factors constitute the consumer behavior, which lays the foundation for developing marketing strategies in the competitive marketplace. It is difficult to learn the perceptions of consumers, as it has high degree of inconsistency and is psychologically complicated. However, consumer cognition is constructed with expectations, emotions, experiences, and derived values. Therefore, companies need to understand consumer cognition analogical to playing building blocks that results into the different dimensions and shapes. Such exercises of building blocks explore opportunities to know consumers and create value for companies to improve their performance in existing markets or break into new markets. Cognitive ergonomics of consumers can be used by companies to measure revenue growth, refine product design to better meet customers' needs, identify customers perceive strengths and weaknesses, and to develop appropriate marketing strategies (Almquist et al. 2016).

Consumers develop semantic map of values while analyzing a product through the available verbal and nonverbal information and build knowledge base to support the decision process. Of many, seven intrinsic factors comprising personality, culture, materialism, shopping tendency, hedonic pleasure, utilitarianism, buying leadership and referrals, and buying impulses are critical to develop customer-centric marketing strategies. Companies need to invest in mapping consumer perceptions in the context of above factors. In addition, socio-cultural and economic perspectives concerning the price, consumer surplus, macro perspectives of products and services also need to be considered by the companies to thoroughly understand consumer psychology. This helps companies in reducing the incidence of consumer defection. Consumers maps their contextual perceptions in mind prior to deriving values and decisions. Such perceptual maps are called perceptual semantics.

Consumers derive their beliefs from the learned culture, self-references, and values perceived from the society and cognitive factors. Consumer perceptions are often agile and need to be endorsed by the peers, friends, and family to support decision making and to put them into practice over a long term. Positive perceptions help consumers believe that corporate promotions are relevant to the attainment of desired goals, the goals for which their impressions are relevant are valuable, and a discrepancy exists between how they want to be perceived and how other people perceive them. A sustainable attitude among consumers leads to cultivate a behavior in due course of time. Experiential marketing helps companies to socialize brands and gain competitive advantage in the marketplace.

Summary

This chapter suggests various managerial strategies to the complexities in the market chaos, entropy, and uncertainties caused due to advancement of technology, growing scope of frugal innovations, and changing consumer preferences. Discussions suggest that companies can develop differentiation strategy in product-mix and position products taxonomically in the markets that demonstrate consumer demand for the differentiated products. This strategy can help customer-centric companies to distinguish product-customer-consumption synergy and can lower the adverse effects of market entropy, demand fragmentation, and customer defection. Accordingly, companies can develop strategies to explore categorical marketing opportunities in emerging, growing, and mature markets over time. The categorical strategies to achieve market competitiveness, which helps companies explore opportunities for growth markets that need efforts to redesign products, extend distribution channels or create new ones.

Companies need to systematically learn competitors' signals and strategies to understand market complexity caused due to the various attributes of competition. Therefore, companies that adapt to such business philosophy choose to operate niche market. It allows to develop consistency in market share, profitability, and business growth. Therefore, the market restructuring appears to be a major challenge to meet the changing business scenarios within the industry and market. Managing the innovation value chain consistently through co-creating commercial innovation ideas, using them to stimulate demand, and diffusing them among the customers and market players help the innovations companies to meet growing challenges of market chaos. Companies engaged in marketing new products based on frugal innovation should explore opportunities by creating high consumer awareness about the cost effectiveness and utilitarian values of the products and services. Consumer judgment, decision making, and behavior depends on cognitive processes that determine the consumer consciousness and buying behavior. Companies can develop marketing strategies on the foundation of consumer ergonomics, consciousness, and underlying emotions.

References

Almquist, E., J. Senior, and N. Bloch. 2016. "The Elements of Value." *Harvard Business Review* 94, pp. 47–53.

Atherton, A. 2007. "Preparing for Business Start-Up: 'Pre-Start' Activities in the New Venture Creation Dynamic." *Journal of Small Business and Enterprise Development* 14, pp. 404–17.

Dawar, N., and C. Bagga. 2015. "A Better Way to Map Brand Strategy." *Harvard Business Review* 93, pp. 90–97.

Govindarajan, V. 2012. "A Reverse-Innovation Playbook." *Harvard Business Review* 90, pp. 120–24.

Hunt, S.D., and S. Madhavaram. 2019. "Adaptive Marketing Capabilities, Dynamic Capabilities, and Renewal Competences: The 'Outside vs. Inside' and 'Static vs. Dynamic' Controversies in Strategy." *Industrial Marketing Management.*

Jungeilges, J., and T. Ryazanova. 2019. "Transitions in Consumption Behaviors in a Peer-Driven Stochastic Consumer Network." *Chaos, Solitons & Fractals* 128, pp. 144–54.

Li, Y., and L. Wang. 2019. "Chaos in a Duopoly Model of Technological Innovation with Bounded Rationality Based on Constant Conjectural Variation." *Chaos, Solitons & Fractals* 128, pp. 116–26.

Liu, X., X. Zhou, B. Zhu, K. He, and P. Wang. 2019. "Measuring the Maturity of Carbon Market in China: An Entropy-Based TOPSIS Approach." *Journal of Cleaner Production* 229, pp. 94–103.

Rajagopal, and A. Rajagopal. 2007. "Competition versus Cooperation: Analyzing Strategy Dilemma in Business Growth under Changing Social Paradigms." *International Journal of Business Environment* 1, pp. 476–87.

Simanis, E., and D. Duncan. 2014. "Profits at the Bottom of the Pyramid." *Harvard Business Review* 92, pp. 86–93.

Soman, D. 2014. "The Innovator's Dilemma: Understanding the Psychology of Adoption." *Rotman Management Magazine*, 5–9.

Waters, G.A. 2009. "Chaos in the Cobweb Model with a New Learning Dynamic." *Journal of Economic Dynamics and Control* 33, pp. 1201–16.

Winter, A., and V. Govindarajan. 2015. "Engineering Reverse Innovations." *Harvard Business Review* 93, pp. 80–89.

About the Author

Rajagopal is a Professor of Marketing at EGADE Business School of Monterrey Institute of Technology and Higher Education (ITESM), Mexico City Campus and Life Fellow of the Royal Society for Encouragement of Arts, Manufacture, and Commerce, London. Dr. Rajagopal is also a Visiting Professor at Boston University, Boston, Massachusetts. He has been listed with biography in various international directories.

He offers courses in the areas of marketing, innovation management, and international business to the students of undergraduate, graduate, and doctoral programs. He has imparted training to senior executives and has conducted over 70 management development programs for the corporate executives and international faculty. Throughout his career, Dr. Rajagopal has delivered a number of courses and executive and doctoral programs in the areas of marketing and international business in various business schools, including the Indian Institute of Management, at Indore and Rohtak, India; Narsee Monjee Institute of Management Studies, Mumbai, India; Institute of Public Enterprise, Hyderabad, India; and International Management Institute, Bhubaneswar, India.

Rajagopal holds post-graduate and doctoral degrees in economics and marketing, respectively, from Ravishankar University in India. He has to his credit 60 books on marketing and innovation management themes and over 400 research contributions that include published research papers in national and international refereed journals. He is the Editor-in-Chief of the *International Journal of Leisure and Tourism Marketing* and *International Journal of Business Competition and Growth*. He is on the editorial board of various journals of international repute. The National Council of Science and Technology (CONACyT), Government of Mexico, by awarding him the honor of the highest level of National Researcher-SNI Level-III, has recognized his research contributions.

He has been awarded UK-Mexico Visiting Chair 2016–2017 for collaborative research on *Global-Local Innovation Convergence* with the University of Sheffield, UK, instituted by the Consortium of Higher Education Institutes of Mexico and the UK.

Index

Letter 'f' after page number indicates figures.

OTHER TITLES IN THE MARKETING COLLECTION

- *Decoding Customer Value at the Bottom of the Pyramid* by Ritu Srivastava
- *Qualitative Marketing Research* by Rajagopal
- *Social Media Marketing* by Alan Charlesworth
- *Employee Ambassadorship* by Michael W Lowenstein
- *Critical Thinking for Marketers, Volume I* by David Dwight and David Soorholtz
- *Critical Thinking for Marketers, Volume II* by David Dwight and David Soorholtz
- *Service Excellence* by Ruth N. Bolton
- *Relationship Marketing Re-Imagined* by Naresh Malhotra and Can Uslay
- *Marketing Plan Templates for Enhancing Profits* by Elizabeth Rush Kruger
- *Launching New Products* by John C. Westman and Paul Sowyrda

Announcing the Business Expert Press Digital Library

Concise e-books business students need for classroom and research

This book can also be purchased in an e-book collection by your library as

- a one-time purchase,
- that is owned forever,
- allows for simultaneous readers,
- has no restrictions on printing, and
- can be downloaded as PDFs from within the library community.

Our digital library collections are a great solution to beat the rising cost of textbooks. E-books can be loaded into their course management systems or onto students' e-book readers. The **Business Expert Press** digital libraries are very affordable, with no obligation to buy in future years. For more information, please visit **www.businessexpertpress.com/librarians**. To set up a trial in the United States, please email **sales@businessexpertpress.com**.